MW01354766

Courtesy Calls Again

in the Family

Judith Fife Mead
&
Marian Therese Horvat, Ph.D.

ISBN: 978-0-9819793-1-1

Library of Congress Number: 2009938366

Printed and bound in the United States of America

Cover: Work by TIA's art desk. The cover reproduces a picture of Queen Astrid and King Leopold of Belgium being greeted by a gentleman at the Brussels World Exhibit of 1935.

Tradition in Action, Inc.
P.O. Box 23135
Los Angeles, CA 90023
www.TraditionInAction.org

Dedicated to our Heavenly Mother,
Our Lady of Good Success,
asking her guidance in directing us to a return
to the Catholic tradition of authentic courtesy
for the restoration of Christendom.

TABLE OF CONTENTS

ILLUSTRATIONS:

* * *

Introduction

In the American Catholic milieu, the call for a restoration of Christian Civilization started as a reaction in the religious sphere. With stunning rapidity after Vatican II, centuries-old traditions had been toppled: The Mass had been rewritten and translated into English, the altars turned around, habits and cassocks abandoned, statues and novenas thrown out, organ and Gregorian chant replaced by guitars and soft rock, Sunday dress downgraded to casual everyday clothing.

After the first shell-shock produced by these radical changes, concerned Catholics began to organize and act in response to the progressivist revolution that seemed intent on the very destruction of the Church. This resistance continues to grow with a dynamism and zeal that the progressivists lack and envy.

Many American supporters of this restoration began to realize that the fight they were making for Catholic tradition should extend beyond the religious sphere. It was not enough to restore the Tridentine Mass if the persons who assisted at it were wearing blue jeans and tank tops, listening to rock music at home, and becoming accustomed to the vulgarities and immoralities of modern entertainment and environments.

These persons, many of them young parents raising families, began to comprehend that the ceremony, hierarchy, and order that they longed to see restored in the Church were also missing in American families, schools, and other institutions. They understood that their fight had to extend further – into the cultural arena. To make a complete cultural counter-revolution would demand restoring and re-civilizing almost all fields of social and cultural life.

Some of these thoughtful Catholics, disillusioned with the myths of the modern world, began to delve more deeply and question the egalitarian myths of America. They looked back in History for a more civilized time as a model to follow. They found that American families and society in general were much more cultured before the Second World War, and even more so before the First Great War. Why? Because at those times they were open to the European cultural influence – that of England, France, Italy, Spain, and Germany, for example.

Insofar as we Americans were open to this healthy influence of the wholesome remnant of Christian Civilization, we expressed some of that spirit by showing ourselves to be well-bred, distinguished, polite, and respectable. To the degree that we rejected those salutary manners of the past, we lost our dignity, self-respect, and seriousness.

The United States became the country of spontaneity and the casual lifestyle. Instead of the civilized people of a great country, we became crass and childish. In the name of joviality and having a good time, almost everything turned to joking, vulgarities, and outright immorality.

Is it possible to restore that good European influence when today Europe itself has adopted the American way of life and followed our crass culture? The answer is still uncertain. By taking the lead in the restoration, perhaps we will give Europeans the courage to reject the bad models we have spread. In any case, the desire for such a restoration is in the air.

This desire has inspired concrete action in the basics of living. Growing numbers of parents are choosing to home-school their children or establish alternative Catholic schools. They are teaching the Baltimore Catechism and studying the History of the Church and Christian Civilization. They are turning off the television in their homes and eschewing the unwholesome entertainments of Hollywood. They are seeking out the sound Catholic customs and traditions of the past and transmitting them to their children in order to build a different and better future.

What is more, they have begun to understand that the Revolution has destroyed a whole way of being and acting – of dressing with distinction, of conversing and speaking with politesse, of carrying oneself and behaving in a dignified way in the family and in society. They are realizing that courtesy and good manners have an important role to play in a Catholic restoration.

Admiring the courtesy of the past, they have begun to grasp a much broader and richer meaning of sacrifice. Maintaining good Catholic customs requires sacrifice.

It is not easy to continually repress what is vulgar, rough, and even offensive in so many of man's impulses. It is easier to slouch on the floor than to sit properly on a sofa or chair. It takes self-control to reflect before speaking, rather than to say whatever comes to mind regardless of the feelings of others. It demands effort to dress properly for every occasion and according to the dignity befitting one's state in life.

How much more convenient it is to wear blue jeans and open shirts to Mass and work, jogging clothes to restaurants and theaters, shorts and t-shirts to shopping centers.

The world around us is moving rapidly toward tribalism, a neo-barbarian way of thinking and living. A turnaround in our own lives is not only possible, but essential. It is the way we must begin to effect the restoration of an authentic Catholic culture.

To be civilized demands both discipline and virtue. Looking toward a brighter tomorrow, a new generation is showing itself willing to make the sacrifices necessary for a life of distinction and refinement. They are responding in a positive way to the ubiquitous call to courtesy that is again beginning to sound.

Understanding courtesy

Frequently, acquiring courtesy is mistakenly confused with learning artificial conventions. A parent cannot simply enroll a youngster in a six-week etiquette class to learn courtesy. Certainly the child will learn some basic directives on which fork and knife to use at a formal dinner, but courtesy encompasses much more than mere conventions.

Courtesy cannot be reduced to a set of rules and table manners to be memorized so that little John or Mary can be self-confident on public occasions. One does not pull good manners out of a drawer like a pair of gloves to be worn at a formal event. Then, when the evening is over, back they go into the box until the next social affair. The utilitarian concept of manners as a means to get ahead in life is not the Catholic courtesy that is being addressed in this small book.

A real return to courtesy requires a broader understanding. Courtesy demands that one show consideration and respect for others. This consideration for others is not an empty formality. It is a consequence of the Catholic mentality that sees in one's neighbor a person who deserves to be treated with seriousness and respect because he was made in the image and likeness of God and was redeemed by the infinitely precious Blood of Christ.

Courtesy encompasses politeness, of course. Well-bred persons should not contradict others in conversation or be clownish. Basic politeness prohibits a guest from criticizing the food or amenities provided. Addressing one's superiors or elders with respect should be second nature to the well-mannered young man or woman. But, courtesy is more than that.

Courtesy is an excellence of the human *convivium* (the way of living together with others), an excellence in the way of being and acting. Pope Pius XII notes that *this excellence in being* of a genteel man or woman reflects a refinement of thought, feeling, soul, and conscience that was inherited from one's forebears and ceaselessly nurtured by the Christian ideal. [1]

It is, he states, an excellence that manifests itself in the "dignity of one's entire bearing and conduct," a dignity, moreover, "that is not imperious, but permits distances to appear in order to inspire in others a higher nobility of soul, mind, and heart."

---

1. Pius XII, *Allocution to the Roman Patriciate and Nobility,* 1945, in Plinio Corrêa de Oliveira, *Nobility and Analogous Traditional Elites in the Allocutions of Pius XII* (York, PA: Hamilton Press,1993), pp. 73-74.

Lastly, he stressed, this excellence reveals itself above all by a superior morality, a righteousness, honesty, and probity that informs every word and every deed. [2]

This is the spirit of courtesy we hope to impart to our readers.

Aims of this work

Chapter I of this work, as a prelude to the more practical guidelines to be set out, presents three important virtues that are prerequisites to the practice of courtesy: humility, justice, and charity.

Perhaps the most challenging chapter of this book is the second, which examines some of the American myths that have fostered egalitarian and erroneous ways of conduct in opposition to the courteous behaviors of the past. Unless we set aside these myths that have generated the modern, casual lifestyle, we cannot become the courteous individuals we should be.

The first place that courtesy must be practiced is within the family. The tone of society is set by the tenor established in the lives of families inside their homes. Therefore, chapters III, IV and V look at the ways proper relationships should be established inside a Catholic family.

How should a husband and wife treat each other and give correct example to their children? What should be the way a father acts with his children? How should a mother train her sons and daughters? By answering these simple, elementary questions, we present the essential elements of sound Catholic relationships within the family unit.

Chapters VI and VII offer some guidelines on proper table manners and the art of conversation in the home.

Much more could be written on the subject, but we have confined ourselves to these topics with the hope that, in this case,

---

2. *Ibid.*

less will be more. That is to say, more people will be encouraged to read our small manual if it does not become an encyclopedia on manners. Our aim is not to present every rule of etiquette, but, rather, to encourage our readers to adopt a more refined, hierarchical, and serious way of being.

If this work on courtesy *in the family* is well-received, we hope in the future to offer another manual that deals with courtesy in relationships with others *in society*.

The apostolate of courtesy

We face here an objection sure to be raised: "What makes you experts on this subject?"

We do not presume to establish ourselves as prototypes of gentility. We are writing this book because we have received insistent requests from several good friends to do so. We searched for a Catholic book dealing with the topic that we could recommend, but we did not find any material that adequately addressed the errors specific to our days.

Therefore, we took up the task of writing this book as a work of apostolate. We present to our readers a model that we are also trying to follow. The good model we hope to transmit is the excellence of Catholic courtesy – the superior fruit of Christian Civilization that still survived in the West until the Cultural Revolution of the '60s.

We have always felt a profound admiration for the goodness, truth, and beauty reflected in the Catholic social order. Comparing our society to that from days past, we became aware that "Lady Courtesy" was inviting us to follow her. Later we realized that this same Lady was inviting more and more people along the same route. This book, then, is an answer to her call.

Our own transformations are far from complete. Habits and spirits that bear the imprint of distinction and perfection cannot be acquired from one day to the next. Often it takes an entire lifetime. But what man alone cannot do, God most certainly can accomplish. He can speed up this process and, with the help of His grace, change us.

We are certain that if we go to Our Lady – with humility and admiration for our glorious past Christian Civilization – she will transform us and make us what we should be. She will give us what we need to become the builders of a new Civilization, the citizens of the Reign of Mary that she promised at Fatima.

This call to courtesy that falls on open ears indicates that its spirit is far from being dead. It is like the plants under the winter snow that lie dormant. When the thaw comes, we see that much of nature is alive. The seeds germinating beneath the snow sprout and become the harvest of tomorrow. It is the promise of a new beginning.

Let us pray that we will correspond to the graces Our Lady is giving in anticipation of the restoration of the Catholic Church and society – and that the thaw will not be too much longer in coming.

* * *

Chapter I

The Virtue of Courtesy

There are some who protest that virtue has nothing to do with courtesy. Prayer, devotions, and pious works make a man advance in the spiritual life, they say – not good manners, protocol, and laws of etiquette.

This position is simply not true. The word "courtesy" derives from the French word for "court" and evokes the superior qualities of character and bearing once expected from persons of noble blood and spirit.

The nobleman had the desire to be exemplary not just in the practice of arms, but in all things – culture, manners, taste, attitudes, and the exemplary practice of Christian virtues. He radiated this brilliance around him like the flame at the tip of a candle. He became a good moral example for the whole social body, stimulating every class to rise in culture, as well as in virtue.

The laws of courtesy were shaped not by sterile etiquette books, but by a spirit of sacrifice and the practice of virtue. We must not be fooled – to live in a refined and dignified manner demands a constant spirit of sacrifice. Our nature revolts against the effort demanded by good manners and protocol. It is much easier to do what we feel like doing, to follow our impulses, to be rough and vulgar.

As a preliminary step to establishing guidelines for relationships and the practice of courtesy in the family, we will present some virtues that support authentic courtesy.

Three main Catholic virtues are prerequisites to the practice of courtesy: humility, justice, and charity.

Humility – accepting our place in the social hierarchy

Humility has an important role to play in the practice of courtesy. Humility is understood here as facing and accepting the truth. It is the honest recognition of one's good qualities, as well as one's shortcomings.

In the social order, humility demands that we present ourselves as neither more nor less than what we are. We practice humility when we know our place in society, acknowledge it, accept it with dignity, and behave accordingly. Humility also demands that we acknowledge the social level, position, and merits of our neighbor and treat him in a manner suitable to what he deserves.

For this reason, the courtesy inspired by Catholic thinking never encourages individuals to aspire to higher social positions than the ones they deserve, but rather urges them to show proper deference to their superiors and a kind protection to their inferiors. Each one remains stably in his own social rank.

This kind of humility is well illustrated by an episode recounted in the stories of old France by Funck Brentano. There was a woodcutter, the head of a family who for many generations had been woodcutters, loyal to the King and France since the time of Charlemagne. King Louis XIV decided to reward such remarkable stability and fidelity. He sent an emissary to the patriarch of the family on his 80th birthday with the message that the King wished to make him a Baron.

The patriarch replied, "I thank His Majesty very much for his gesture, but I respectfully decline the honor. I prefer to remain the first woodcutter of France rather than the least of its Barons."

It is an incident rich in teachings about social humility. This man, with a profound sense of his own identity, had a legitimate pride in being who he was, without the anxiety or ambition of the social climber. We can appreciate this story, particularly when we see it in contrast to the modern anxiety and instability that accompany the fast-lane career track adopted by so many ambitious men and women in our times.

Most of us have heard many sermons on how it is prideful to put on artificial airs and pretend to be higher socially than we really are. More difficult for us to grasp is the realization that it is also prideful when we pretend to be socially lower than we are.

If Queen Elizabeth of England would start to appear in T-shirts, blue jeans, and moccasins, she would be revolting against the secular dignity of the Monarchy – an act of pride. Similarly, when we want to appear in public in a way that is not keeping with our social rank, we commit an act of pride.

Therefore, the social virtue of humility requires each one to accept his place in society and acknowledge it by an appropriate behavior, dress, and way of being.

Justice – giving each one the treatment he deserves

Along with humility, courtesy demands the practice of justice. A basic axiom of Roman Law – valid for all times – is that each one should be given what he has a right to receive.

Because people are unequal in status, situation, intelligence, and talent, the necessity of justice demands unequal treatment. It is the practice of justice, not just consideration for others or mere protocol, that demands we offer the form of respect and attention to which one has a right.

Justice demands that a professor at a university be treated by his students with a deference indicating his superiority. The student should stand when the professor enters the classroom, open the door for him, allow him to enter the room first, and listen politely without interruption to what he presents. Analogously, at a university banquet, justice requires that the same professor address the university rector with a title of respect, step back to let him enter first, and defer naturally to him as a superior.

Flagrant injustices can be noted today not only in classrooms, but also in the family, where so often children do not give their parents the respectful treatment they deserve.

Often the first reaction of many Americans is to recoil from situations involving the question of who is greater or lesser because of the deeply rooted principle that all men should be treated equally. What is true and what is false in this principle?

It is true that since we are all equal in essence, we deserve a certain basic treatment that is essentially equal: Each man deserves to be treated with the respect due to his natural human dignity. But since the accidents of birth, position, talent, nature, and personality are not equal, men deserve to be treated differently, in an unequal way, according to those accidents.

Therefore, the principle that everyone should be treated equally is an unjust principle, a revolutionary principle that promotes the destruction of the innate hierarchy that exists in society and in the natural order created by God.

To the contrary, courtesy is the happy tribute we pay to one another in recognizing not only our essential equality – the likeness of God in every soul – but also the different characteristics God gave each of us.

It is a great good to know how to treat a person above you in a manner appropriate to his position. And, vice-versa, the superior who knows how to treat those under him exercises an action of justice that supports good order in society and gives glory to God.

The rules of military courtesy still reflect this salutary mutual respect for authority and justice proper to hierarchical social bodies.

Enlisted personnel always address officers and civilian officials as "Sir" as a title of respect. The conversation of officers on duty is instructed to be formal, out of respect for their position of responsibility, as well as for their personnel.

Titles are used regularly: "Major Brown, have you already read the document General Taylor sent us?" "Yes, Colonel McKinney, I have." It should not be this: "Hey Joe, did you take a look at that draft Ted sent us?" "Yeah, Bill."

When an officer enters a room, the enlisted men stand at attention until signaled otherwise. The inferior officer always walks and sits to the left of his seniors, a custom that originated in the times of chivalry. Because the shield was carried on the left arm, the defensive side, the subordinate took his place there to show that he was ready to defend his superior.

When Catholic principles were applied concretely in society, a person's dignity used to correspond to his station and rank, and then the formula of respect and honor was in accord with the merits and rights of each.

At universities, hats were taken off fully for professors, but were raised halfway for tutors. At dances and balls, the highest ranking figure present was accorded the right of presiding. At the first Philadelphia Assembly, for example, the Governor selected one of the ladies and opened the dance. At banquets and dinners, ceremonious entrance processions were formed according to the hierarchical importance of each guest. There were even titles of respect for addressing one's mother and father.

For a man with the Catholic spirit, the hierarchical order is a kind of oxygen that permits him to breathe.

Charity – respecting ourselves and others

The practice of courtesy also requires the virtue of charity.

If only justice prevailed in the treatment of our fellowman, social life would be too harsh. Did Mr. Sullivan commit an embarrassing *gaffe*? Rather than chastise him for his error, we ignore it and treat him well. Is Mrs. Williams too loquacious? Instead of rolling our eyes sarcastically, we smile politely and listen to her chatter. Are the Browns over-praising the supposed qualities of their children? Instead of pointing out the exaggerations, we smile and acquiesce. This is not theatrical or hypocritical behavior – it is charity.

Such charity is, of course, learned and practiced at home. Courteous behavior requires one to control his moods and govern his actions. Imagine a family dinner where everyone is concerned about being agreeable and pleasing the others around the table. Then imagine a lifetime of such evenings – now you have an idea of the Catholic courtesy of times past.

A civilized man presents himself with all the dignity and decorum that his social condition requires. Doing this, he demonstrates the respect he has for himself and the respect he has for God, in Whose presence he is always placed. Each one of us is worthy of respect, for we were created in the image and likeness of God. Therefore, in charity and justice toward ourselves, we must present ourselves in accordance with this dignity in our homes, even if we are alone.

But we also have an obligation of charity and justice toward our neighbor. We owe him respect also. To treat our neighbor well is something we do because we want to show him goodness and because he has the right to receive a dignified treatment. He is also made in the image and likeness of God.

Even appropriate dress relies in part on the law of charity, that one should show respect for others. If a man does not dress well, according to his age and position in society, it signifies a mark of contempt for others.

The charity governing courtesy has a beautiful aspect. At times, as we have already noted, it transcends justice and requires that we close our eyes to the defects and transgressions of others and act as if they do not exist. At other times courtesy demands that we give consideration to a person who, strictly speaking, does not merit our charity or regard.

Let us consider the case of a man who has offended another in the past and now needs his help. If the offended party closes his eyes to the past insult and assists the one who injured him, he acts in the spirit of charity. He is not obliged by justice to offer help, but in many cases it may be the noble thing to offer assistance as an act of charity.

We can see this in the treatment of the Church toward souls. One of her most charming harmonic contrasts is her militancy against sin and evil and, at the same time, her goodness that manifests itself in the great courtesy and care she displays toward souls.

For example, in the confessional the priest often used to invoke the highest motives to help the soul accept the correction: "My son, Our Lord Jesus Christ suffered and shed His Precious Blood to purchase the pardon of our sins. He did this personally for you because He wants you to be with Him for all eternity. Take this into consideration, and make the firm purpose not to sin again."

By her example, the Church teaches us to treat others with greater goodness than they merit.

Blessed Raymond de Lull's book of chivalry

After spending his youth at the court of the King of Aragon, at age 30 Raymond de Lull became a Third Order Franciscan. One of the many works he wrote was a book on the Order of Chivalry. The qualities Lull considered requisite for a knight were a combination of martial arts and Catholic virtues, with an emphasis placed on the latter.

A knight had to be brave, strong of body, and skilled in the use of arms. More important, he had to be disposed to defend the Holy Church and his King. Devotion to the Church led him to practice justice and charity in a particular way by protecting its special charges – women, widows, orphans, and all the weak and helpless.

The knight also had to be courteous to all and to keep himself well-armed and well-dressed out of respect for himself and his high station. He had to abjure perjury and lies, while remaining humble and chaste. At the end of his work, Lull listed the virtues and vices, showing how the former were necessary to the true knight, while the latter destroyed him.

The popularity of Lull's book inspired many translations and adaptations. Chivalry became synonymous with courtesy. A gentleman in French is actually called a *chevalier*, coming from *Chevalerie*, the French word for Chivalry.

Courtesy, this exquisite flower of the virtues of justice, charity, and humility, gave to life what the French so aptly term the *douceur de vivre*, the sweetness of life. Those whom courtesy is calling today would like, once again, to taste this sweetness in their daily lives. A first step toward this goal is to recognize that the laws of courtesy are intricately connected to the practice of virtue.

* * *

Chapter II

American Myths and Models

Now that we have shown that the authentic practice of virtue is required to observe the laws of courtesy inspired by Christian Civilization, our next step is to acknowledge and begin to combat the American myths that stand in the way of its practice.

What do we mean by myth?

When we mention myth, we are referring to a particular concept that captivates the admiration of a group and becomes a psychological model for that group. A family, a region, a state, or a whole people can have its own myth. For example, a celebrated war hero can become a larger-than-life model for the sons and nephews of a whole family to emulate. Daniel Boone, with his frontier exploits, came to personify the pioneer and hunter with his frontier exploits, first for the state of Kentucky, and then for the whole country.

The myth is normally a social and moral ideal, presented by certain literature and art, that seeks to represent aspects of the psychology of a people. As noted above, a myth is often personified in a human type, either a real person or an imaginary one.

The legendary figure of the *cowboy*, for example, constitutes the model of a human type embodied in a myth that represents an important component of the American spirit. This myth was created largely by Hollywood. It is represented by John Wayne standing tall in the saddle – the rugged, free, self-reliant, and taciturn man. The myth is not necessarily the *reality* of the cowboy. It is the model and lifestyle that he represents in the minds of the people.

The *torero*, or bullfighter, represented a model for a considerable part of Spain. He was the man who, with art, elegance, and agility, enjoyed challenging death while he proved his superiority over the fierce bull. Sadly, most of modern Spain has rejected the challenges and heroism of the past.

Its new model could be represented by Sancho Panza, the plump shield-bearer of Don Quixote, whose ideal was to avoid risk and enjoy a mediocre life filled with small pleasures. Such a change of models and myths explains much about contemporary Spain.

Taming the myths

Myths exert a strong influence on society. Some sociologists affirm that they play a central role in developing the identity of a people and shaping the social order.

We can either go along with a myth or reject it. Once we are aware of a myth's influence on our own family or society, we can try to eliminate it (if it is bad) or foster it (if it is good). It is a challenge to face a myth, just as it is a challenge to face the wind. The myth blows here and there and causes good or bad effects. The skillful sailor tames the wind and makes it work for him to bring his ship to the good port. This should be our aim as well: to tame and conquer the myths that shape our way of being so we can develop good states of spirit that will help us to practice virtue and reach Heaven.

A man or woman who earnestly responds to the call to courtesy must, as a first step, valiantly evaluate the myths that contradict courtesy and support the egalitarian customs dominating most of our ambiences.

In order to pave the way for the practice of courtesy, we will expose some of the most influential myths that have helped to fashion a casual, egalitarian, and discourteous American way of life.

Here is the challenge we present to each of our readers: Face the myth that applies to you or your family, and then begin to counter it in your daily actions.

The *natural man*

The notion that nature is good and civilization is bad – based on the erroneous thinking of Rousseau – is deeply rooted in the American spirit. According to this false theory, if we were to just leave man in nature, he would be fine. It is civilization – along with its formality and protocol – that have robbed man of his primitive innocence. Left to himself, without these false constraints of society, the *natural man* would always do what is right and good.

This myth is particularly strong in the California mentality, where everything that is natural, casual, and relaxed is lauded – nay, revered! For example, the California *beach boy* is one of the models that circulates this myth. He is the youth who surfs and parties on the beach, camping out and enjoying nature. He is no stranger to free-love and drugs, and prefers to live from handouts from his parents or from occasional jobs.

In the false vision of life of the *natural man*, the laws of courtesy appear as a barrier to the happy mingling of equals. The *natural man* boasts a hatred of manners because he abhors everything artificial. He extols the supposed "virtues" of informality that in his view reflect sincerity and equality and generate creativity. For him, any type of protocol stands for restraints and restrictions on his natural inclinations.

It is not difficult to see that such presuppositions provide the *natural man* the excuse he needs to say and do whatever he wants whenever he chooses.

To say exactly what one pleases, however, can often wound, anger, and belittle others. It also gives one a self-dictated permission to use slang, coarse language, and even profanities.

To do as one likes is often to do what others dislike. The man who follows this myth thinks he should be able to wear what he likes, without consideration of his neighbor or respect for Morals or the laws of basic decency.

The young man who cannot resist the fashion to wear low-rider shorts that reveal his buttocks does not consider how this fad repulses those who are subjected to the spectacle.

The young woman who considers being fashionable more important than following Catholic Morals imagines it is beautiful to wear pants and tops that reveal her bare belly and hips. She blithely disregards the old-fashioned critics. She assumes she has the right to wear whatever she wants since she is not hurting anyone. However, her naturalist attitude does harm – not only the sensibilities of others who maintain some sense of modesty and refinement, but also the standards of a civilized Catholic society.

Apparently the *natural man* simply wants to be informal and free. He prefers to just live and let live. In reality, his way of thinking virtually requires that everyone else be like him. If he meets someone who is refined or reserved, the *natural man* accuses him of being fake, proud, and arrogant. That is, there is an imperialist tinge to the myth of the *natural man.*

Hollywood is filled with examples of this type of person. Daily we are bombarded with photos of actors dining in top restaurants wearing t-shirts, jeans, and flip-flops, accompanied by women in tank tops and shorts. Americans hardly need a longer introduction to this type of man or woman, so extolled in movies and literature.

Today the secular media and the progressivist Church are exalting the primitive so-called *natural* lifestyle of natives as the quintessence of "pure" living. In this reinterpretation of history, the Catholic missionaries are those who arrogantly imposed an artificial civilization and repressive customs on the noble savage. The aim is to reach a new 21st century tribalism, where Indians are presented as the perfect model.

Persons who take the myth of the *natural man* as a model adopt a false vision of life since, fundamentally, they reject the existence of original sin. Furthermore, they reject the splendor of culture and civilization – the excellent fruits of the preaching of the Catholic Church and the Redemption of Our Lord.

The *spontaneous man*

The myth of spontaneity celebrates the man who reacts immediately to new social situations with an optimistic impulse – without reflection or any second thought.

Since this first impulse supposedly reflects sincerity and frankness, it justifies setting aside conventions. On this particular point, both myths – the *natural man* and the *spontaneous man* – are similar. The criticisms regarding the first apply to the second as well. But there are also marked differences between them.

While the myth of the *natural man* presents models of persons who are usually outside society (loners, often somewhat misanthropic), the man who embraces the myth of *spontaneity* is usually sociable, boisterous, and quick to joke and fool around.

Since he is sociable, the *spontaneous man* generally knows some rules of society – just enough to break them jovially and impose his own conventions. He may still wear a jacket, shirt, and tie, but, as soon as he can, he takes off the jacket, unbuttons the collar, and loosens the tie. At a party, he seats himself and nonchalantly crosses his feet on a coffee table. After dinner, with no care for the ladies and gentlemen present and no hesitance to set a bad example for the children, he lies down on the sofa to take a rest.

People laugh at him and excuse his extravagance: "Ah! You know Mike. He does what he feels like doing…"

The typical *spontaneous man* is often successful in business. In fact, he believes this success gives him the liberty to more easily break the social rules. When he speaks, he is loud and likes to bring attention to himself. If a lady enters the circle, our spontaneous man blurts out, "Libby, are you dieting, or have you become anorexic? You look like a skeleton! Man, you could use a little flesh on those bones!"

Now if the lady also follows the myth of *spontaneity,* she will not be offended or embarrassed. Instead she replies: "Poor Mike, you're as stupid as ever! Or maybe you're becoming blind because I haven't lost a pound since I last saw you." Everyone laughs at the exchange of two spontaneous individuals challenging one another.

Our corresponding *spontaneous lady* feels free to slip in and out of her shoes while talking. In the middle of a conversation with a group of people, her back feels stiff, so she stretches both arm out, with an extravagantly wide gesture to ease the tension. If someone is giving a talk to a small group and there are no more chairs available, she sits on the floor cross-legged (Indian-fashion) and follows the account with an assumed serious air.

Once we were at a shopping center and saw a group of young women. They were walking toward a store when one of them suddenly began to dance, raising her arms in the air, twirling and snapping her fingers to some imaginary music. No one seemed to think anything of her unconventional behavior. She was simply celebrating her spontaneity, doing what moved her at the moment.

But why should we be surprised by the prevalence of such behavior, when the spontaneous man and woman are glorified today in the majority of television sit-coms and movies produced by Hollywood?

The myth of *spontaneity* generates extravagance. For example, we read a piece of society news on a charity ball in Paris where the guest of honor was an American movie star. The dress was formal, ladies in long gowns and men in black tie. The American guest of honor showed up in a tuxedo, but wearing white tennis shoes...

There were no complaints, just smiles. After all, he is an American... What more can you expect from those spontaneous people? Our nation has become synonymous with extravagance.

This regrettable fame has a long history. An early model for young women of this kind of extravagant spontaneity was Alice Roosevelt, who was 17 when her father, Theodore, became President in 1901. Beautiful and with an aristocratic bearing, she nonetheless had a complete disregard for social convention and took pleasure in shocking the "staid" Washington society with her extraneous exploits and spontaneous actions.

Her popularity spread worldwide, as a fawning media followed her entourage on her trips to Europe and the Far East and enthusiastically reported her unpredictable flights of fancy: learning hula dancing in Hawaii, jumping fully clothed into a makeshift pool on the deck of a ship, making startling off-the-cuff comments to dignified personages, using improper slang and smoking cigarettes in polite company.

Many young women sought to mimic her spontaneous and extravagant way of being, enjoying the sensation of challenging convention.

Why does the spontaneous person clash with the courtesy generated by Christian Civilization? Basically, the myth of *spontaneity* is the glorification of unbridled reactions and sensations, leaving a person free from the restrictions of any hierarchical order, consistent logic, or upright moral code.

The *big boy*

From our country's earliest history, the American woman established an almost complete sovereignty over social life and behavior. This was in contrast to the European scene, where courtiers, noblemen, and statesmen dominated in the social life and where men were the indisputable head of families.

In Europe it was men, not women, who wrote the courtesy manuals instructing others on gentility and refined behavior. In America it was different. It was the women who generally regulated the style of living, dispensed hospitalities, and managed society.

Regarding protocol, in the early 19th century women became the authors of a slew of etiquette manuals intended not only to refine themselves, but also to improve their husbands and sons. Instead of men at the helm of the social sphere, it was women – telling men how to dress, eat, dance, talk, and help a lady into the car. For the American man, social life, etiquette, and manners belonged to the world of women. Perhaps this is why protocol is not taken very seriously in United States.

American women began to exercise the authority in the home, thereby generating the tendency for the American man to take on the appearance of a *big boy*, another young rascal for his mother/ wife/sister to chide and put in order.

In their desire to glorify youth, Hollywood and the media have accentuated this inclination for men to be *big boys.* More and more men have avoided seriousness and maturity. Abandoning their topcoats and the discreet colors and serious style of clothes typical of the mature age, grown men of every profession – politicians, professors, and bankers, as well as carpenters and clerks – have begun to dress, talk, and adopt the mannerisms of their sons and nephews. Instead of representing the authority of the family, the father has begun to look and act like a *big boy* – joking, nonchalant, superficial, unreflective, and given to a certain brash spontaneity.

Today it is plain to see that many men, who should be responsible for maintaining the good sense and equilibrium of the family and society, act and look like *big boys*. The venerable patriarch of the past, respected for his experience, wisdom, keen discernment, and strength of soul, is replaced by the foolish figure of a perpetual youth in pursuit of pleasure.

If men would firmly reject the *big boy* myth and assume their proper roles – insisting on the correct protocol in their homes and assuming command of the family social life – we believe our country would be well on its way to a return to courtesy.

The *cowboy* and the *pioneer woman*

The human type of the *cowboy* (which we mentioned earlier in the chapter) and his counterpart, the *pioneer woman,* had courage, decisiveness, and a sense of sacrifice. Our country owes a considerable part of its expansion into the West and the South to these two human types.

These two ideals manifested themselves in particular ways. The *cowboy* was determined, uncommunicative, living a precarious life in the saddle or on his ranch. He wore his boots, hat, and red bandanna as a uniform, accompanied by his guns, dog, and tobacco. He was satisfied with a staple meal of beans, bacon and biscuits and the basic rudiments of hygiene. Simultaneously he was the adventurer – facing Indians and bandits, enduring desert heat and mountain snow. He would set out on the cattle trail to drive his herd from Wyoming to California, prepared to meet untold dangers along the way.

The mate of this rustic he-man, the *pioneer woman*, was likewise simple in tastes and needs, capable of grabbing a musket and fending off Indians alongside her man. Tough and hardened by the harsh, solitary life in the wilderness, she was man enough to run the ranch when her *cowboy* was out on a drive.

The myth of the *cowboy* – courage, adventure, rusticity, an uncomplicated justice often worked by one's own hands – has enthused many generations of Americans and is still alive. As we have already mentioned, the lasting popularity of John Wayne, the classic hero of cowboy stories in Hollywood films, is evidence of this general admiration.

These rustic models, however, stand in direct opposition to the models of a gentleman and a lady. In the normal development of a Catholic country, the *cowboy* naturally should develop a finer discernment, more cultivated tastes, more polished conversation, and an appreciation for culture and art. Similarly, the *pioneer woman* should set aside her tough, masculine ways, refine her manners, hire tutors to teach her children music and art, and decorate her home in a more cultivated way.

In fact, in some measure, this progression did take place. Today Los Angeles, San Francisco, Dallas, Houston, and Denver are respected centers of culture, art, music, and technology.

The myth of the *cowboy* and the *pioneer woman* did not die, however; they remain firmly entrenched in the American mentality. For many, adopting this myth provides the excuse to reject good manners and refinement as the superfluous niceties of what is considered a phony civilization. Self-reliant cowboys can make their own rules – an attitude that appeals to many. They can even make their own religion, as evidenced by the "cowboy chuches" that are sprouting up throughout the country.

Also implied is the notion that our rough *cowboy* is more masculine than the civilized city gentleman. This view, in our opinion, is an empty pretension. We do not see how any cowboy could be more brilliantly courageous than a *French musketeer,* who was cultivated and highly refined in manners. Could a cowboy be more relentlessly intrepid than a *German military officer,* whose aristocratic spirit shone in both his disciplined demeanor and admiration for the arts and philosophy? And who could be more terrible in attack than a *Japanese samurai,* with his unabashed love for delicate things and artistic performance of martial arts conceived as intricate dances?

No, it is preposterous for our *cowboy* to imagine he is more masculine than the civilized models of other peoples just because he is rough and rude. It is merely an excuse to continue to practice his more comfortable, less disciplined, and essentially egalitarian habits.

The *Puritan model*

The myths we are listing have their roots in two basic models: the Puritan and the Individualist. Both of these types have instilled a mindset on the American spirit that defies the laws of courtesy and refinement we should have inherited from our European ancestors.

The English Puritans who landed in our country were members of one of the most egalitarian Protestant factions, the Quakers. As everyone knows, there are many different fragments that are gathered under the general name of Protestantism.

First there are the Anglicans and Lutherans, who deny the Pope but recognize Bishops. Then there are the Presbyterians, who deny the Pope and Bishops but acknowledge priests. Finally, we find the Anabaptists, who deny the Pope, Bishops, and the Clergy, that is, the entire religious hierarchy. They believe that all religious power comes directly from the people. Their ministers are merely the delegates of the almighty faithful. The Puritans who landed in our country were part of this last, most radical sector.

Not only were the Puritans opposed to religious hierarchy, but they hated all pomp, ceremony, and richness in worship. They considered all these so-called extraneous things as "corrupt." Hence their name – the "puritans," the pure ones. They built stark, cold temples, stripped of any element of art, and in them they executed the simplest liturgy possible.

The Puritans extended this same false idea of poverty and hatred for ceremony and refinement to all aspects of human life. All accoutrements of refinement – fine clothing and jewelry, high quality furniture and objects of art, beautiful silver tea services, finely painted china, crystal goblets – were presented as frivolities that drew people away from God.

Everything that pertained to hierarchy of rank was likewise deemed offensive because it could lead to pride. Following their fundamentally egalitarian position, the Puritans wrongly believed that the defense of one's social position presupposes scorn or lack of consideration for others.

Finally, good manners and genteel conversation were presented as a needless and effeminate byproducts of the degenerate

Rome-dominated civilization. All these "extras" had to be rejected in order to be "pure."

During the struggle for American independence, as the colonies sought to free themselves from the English Monarchy, Puritanism married Democracy. To be independent – to be American – became synonymous with being uncivilized.

This mentality was expressed, for example, in the play *The Contract*, a dramatic condemnation of European gentility. The production was a great hit when it was first performed in New York City in 1787. In it, the effeminate Billy Dimple, educated in a fine school and master of the polite arts, seems ridiculous next to Colonel Manly, the plain and forthright revolutionary patriot.[3]

The message is simple: Good European manners are unmanly and unnecessary. What better suits the egalitarian American ideology are simple clothes, honest values, plain talk, and hard work.

A genre of popular fiction grew up in 19th century America encouraging this ideology through sentimental stories about young women and men who adopted plain dress and manners after discovering religion.

One heroine of these "conversion stories" in *The Christian Parlor Book* was Laura. Before she found religion, Laura was worldly and vain, with her "ringlets like serpents," jewelry, stylish clothing and light demeanor. But finally she realized the folly of her ways and fully embraced Puritanism. She fixed her hair in tight braids, threw off all her jewelry, and chose a somber dress.

There would be no more outings, cards, parties, wine, or fancy food for Laura. Now she understood that any show of genteel living and cavalier courtesy were signs of worldliness that

---

3. Richard L. Bushman, *The Refinement of America* (New York: Vintage House, 1992), p. 193.

engendered pride. Courtly manners and refinement were artificial impositions – obstacles to the American Puritan lifestyle.[4]

This opposition to mannerly refinement deeply penetrated the American spirit, even among the genteel element of our country.

Such a myth persists in the American psyche, even in the Catholic milieu. Partly in reaction to the extravagance and immorality of the modern lifestyle and partly because of this deep-seated suspicion of genteel "trappings," some Catholics imagine that holiness requires the rejection of everything beautiful and elegant in the temporal sphere. They wrongly believe that the way to escape the evil of the modern day world is to rid themselves of everything civilized and refined.

These Catholics do not realize the inherent contradiction in their position: While they clamor for a return of ceremony, beauty, splendor, and hierarchy in the religious sphere, they renounce its natural reflection and extension in the temporal sphere.

In this book we advocate the return of gentility to counter the Puritan model. We maintain that it is time to show that we can be both American and civilized. The good customs of Christian Civilization – far from drawing us away from God – will bring us closer to Our Lord and Our Lady.

The *individualist*

When we criticize the *individualist* model, we are not speaking of the individualism that is the proper and healthy development of one's personality – that which makes a person a unique and individual reflection of God. Nor are we speaking of the rich sense of individuality that a group of people preserve in regional cultures, one of the healthiest and most charming aspects of a Christian Civilization.

---

4. *The Christian Parlor Book: Devoted to Science, Literature and Religion* (New York, 1853), pp. 17-24.

The *individualist* of which we speak is a byproduct of modern democracies with their exaggerated idea of liberty. It is the spirit that reacts against the supposed restraints on personal liberty that the laws of courtesy require.

According to Catholic Morals, personal liberty is the autonomy to choose the means of doing what is good and of serving God. This is what true liberty is.

As one can see, it is quite different from the modern liberalism of our democracies, whereby each one has the right to do whatever he wants, as long as it does not harm his neighbor. This is a relativist principle, valid only if everyone is good. If your neighbor is bad, he can – and will – do inconsiderate and even evil things, proclaiming this to be his right in the name of liberty.

In society, however, a man should not be free to do evil. Nor should he be free to do whatever he wants. This version of freedom constitutes an abuse of liberty that facilitates, among other things, the birth of the *individualist*. Essentially, the individualist only cares about himself. He is fundamentally an egoist.

This false idea of liberty is deeply anchored in our American mentality. Often in its name we reject a more dignified social behavior and its correspondent rules of protocol.

In the name of *individualism,* a teenager demands the right to pierce his nose, tattoo his arm, dye his hair green, and wear a long black overcoat. "Don't cramp my style," he snarls to his parents in his contention to be "himself." Basically, he is demanding a kind of kingship that allows him to transgress any convention or rule of behavior, without being restricted by a moral rule of life.

What the *individualist* does not realize is that there is someone behind the scene controlling the punk styles he follows. Our *individualist* does not recognize that he is not a model of originality; he actually is a slave to the current fashions. He mindlessly follows the latest fad that makes him look like everyone else. He does what he wants, imagining himself to be unique, a Thoreautype acting out his civil disobedience in his own Walden. What he does not want to do, of course, is to follow the manners and customs of Christian Civilization.

The myth of individualism inspired the hippie revolution in dress and manners of the '60s, when youth claimed their supposed right to live without rules of protocol or status: "I want to wear this, to act like this, to be free of everything representing any class. I have the right to follow my own caprices. My right of *individuality* demands it."

A lie never gives an honest fruit, and this false claim of *individuality* has resulted, ironically enough, in a radical conformity to a second-rate, vulgar type of man who lacks the great personality and character of figures from times past. An egalitarian society of radical *individualists* produces social mediocrity, or worse.

On the other hand, one of the blessed fruits of a hierarchical society is the production of a superior human type and a society replete with rich personalities and diverse and colorful character types.

Egalitarianism – the root cause

Underlying all these false notions of conduct and ways of being is a revolutionary egalitarianism, which claims that every social difference is evil and social equality is good. This ideology has been spreading everywhere from the birth of our country until today.

Unfortunately, many American Catholics have been strongly influenced by this false ideology.

What is being forgotten is basic Catholic catechism. God created the world as a hierarchy with harmonious relationships so that the ensemble of creation would reflect His infinite perfection. Therefore, as part of this grand plan, society should be hierarchical and have harmonious dealings among its classes so that it will also reflect God and give Him glory.

The good relationships among different classes require the good rapport among the individuals of each of these classes, who, in their turn, are also different from each other. Good manners, refinement of behavior, and proper protocol are the means developed by Catholic cultures to accomplish these harmonious bonds. Thus, they are ways to mirror God, as well as to love and serve Him.

We cannot insist enough on the importance of recognizing that the egalitarian spirit is the greatest enemy of courtesy. It hates everything that makes one person superior to another in every sphere. It demands that the citizen be equal to the King, the layman equal to the Bishop, and the child equal to the parent. Consequently, all the symbols, titles and traditions that reflect these inequalities must be abolished.

As the reader can see, by observing modern society and culture, this egalitarianism has gone far in imposing itself on our customs and way of life – and it would like to go even further. How can we stop its progress?

A necessary first step is to recognize this egalitarian spirit for the evil that it is, refuse to follow its dictates, and return to the practice of the courtesy and protocol of the past.

In the end, we have a confrontation of two philosophies of life: egalitarianism, which generates vulgarity, and hierarchy, which generates refinement.

It is to invite you to refinement that we have written this book.

* * *

Chapter III

The Husband and the Wife

Before offering some suggestions for courtesy in the day-to-day life of spouses, let us look at how the role of love in marriage has changed in Western society. We will look at three concepts of marriage – the Catholic, the Romantic, and the one fostered by the Cultural Revolution.

In a Catholic marriage, love is the mutual esteem between spouses, born from a realistic sharing of the same ideals. The husband and wife want to give glory to God, raise a family, and save their souls and the souls of their children. They choose each other without romantic illusions. They like each other and admire the good qualities they see in one another. They know that they will face many sufferings and have decided to endure these trials together. They promise before God to be faithful to one another until death.

It is a wise concept where reason commands more than emotion, although the legitimate sentiments and affection certainly have their place as well. The union based on this concept normally is stable and lasts until death.

For Romanticism, love is an affinity of souls that comes from mutual sentiments of love. He desires her and vice-versa, with an intensity of emotions that is close to ecstasy.

"We fell in love," they explain. When this happens, everything is supposed to stop and fall into place. It does not matter that there is a difference of religions and psychologies, that they are from dissimilar social backgrounds, that they have different expectations about raising a family. Because they are in love, they should blindly obey its imperative call.

Certainly this intense sentiment can last for a while, but it is a wild bird that is very difficult to tame and keep caged forever. It escapes and flies away after a certain period of time, and the spouses begin to live in a sad nostalgia for those first moments. Or worse, after a time he – or she – begins to feel those same intense sentiments for another person…

If love is a magic call from destiny, as Romanticism imagines, how is the problem of a new love that comes into one's life resolved? It is simple. The solution is to follow the call and leave aside the first conjugal partner. It is a censurable solution, of course, which produces instability in the institution of marriage and causes enormous sufferings and tragedies.

In Romanticism, love is really egoism. It is two people turned to their own sentimental pleasure –fundamentally an egocentric position. The union based on this concept is destined to be short or unhappy.

For the Cultural Revolution, love is reduced primarily to a sexual attraction. The relationship based on it lasts as long as the animal instincts are aroused. The partners change according to the circumstances. As we can see, this last corrosion is one of the final steps of the Revolution before reaching the goal of general free-love and the total destruction of marriage.

Marriages made today can follow any of these three concepts, but usually there is some blend, with an unlimited possibility of mixtures. For example, a couple may have the first intention of following Catholic Morals and establishing a stable family. However, because the wife harbored romantic illusions about their life together, she may experience great disappointments. Unless she embraces the cross she was not expecting and makes the decision to remain together, even without that perfect "happiness," then the marriage can end in a divorce.

Or perhaps the husband has the vulgar customs and corrupted morals of the Cultural Revolution. He marries, promising to reform. But before long the fires of passion wane, and he tires of the effort demanded by a stricter moral code and higher standards. His eye begins to wander, and he returns to his vices and crude ways, ready for the first excuse to leave a relationship that has become staid and boring. The prospects for this marriage are bleak indeed.

It is up to each couple to avoid the wrong concepts of love and to stay with the sound Catholic one. The vigilant Catholic parents will also form their children to have the proper expectations of marriage and will steer them away from young men and women with false ideas.

Courtesy between the husband and the wife

The Catholic Church teaches us that man was created to rule visible creation for the glory of God, and woman was created to be his companion and helpmate.

This simple statement sets the tone not only for the relationship between husband and wife, but also for a social life where the man should govern external things and the woman should create conditions for him to do so with as much ease as possible. Often the husband, rather than relying solely on his own judgment, will ask the assistance and advice of his wife.

On the subject of courtesy, this general rule translates in many different ways. The first thing that one notes about conjugal life in a Catholic home is that everything – the ways of being, acting, speaking, and dressing – should nourish the development of a profound seriousness in both the husband and wife in considering their individual missions in life.

We realize that such seriousness and mutual respect have characteristics that are quite opposed to modern sentiments and lifestyles. We also know that this attitude is a necessary element that must be restored for things to be set aright.

Mutual respect for high reasons

The husband should be the source of authority and treated as such. This is the key to a stable Catholic relationship. If the husband and wife adopt the modern idea that they are equal in authority, they build on shifting sands. Even if a woman is more talented or energetic, this does not make her more capable of governing the family and making the final decisions for it.

A Spanish Cardinal in the last century gave this sound advice to husbands: "Men, be men. You are the head of the family. You are for your wife as Christ is for the Church, according to the Apostle Paul.

"Your *first right* is your pre-eminence in the family ... Your *first duty* is to recollect yourself and consider how to exercise this principal responsibility and to live in a way in which you are constantly conscious of your dignity."[5]

His wise counsel – far from outdated – sets important guidelines to establish a courteous relationship between a Catholic husband and wife:

- The husband is always conscious of his authority and behaves in a way befitting it. He sets the standards for the family by following good customs and forbidding vulgar or coarse manners, language, and dress in his home. He assumes the responsibility of establishing a Catholic culture not only in the laws and institutions of society, but, first of all, in his own home. The wife respects and admires his authority as God-given and part of the natural order.

- The husband is also aware that he must exercise this authority with an authentic respect and consideration for his wife, his natural companion and the mother of his children. For this reason, regardless of his moods or feelings, he is courteous to her in their day-to-day interaction.

This mutual respect and admiration is the foundation for a harmonious family life. A woman should feel herself respected as a wife and mother so that she can make the admirable effort of maintaining a well-ordered and welcoming home. A man should

---

5. Cardinal Isidro Gomá y Tomás, *La Familia, según el derecho natural y cristiano* (Barcelona: Rafael Casulleras, 1952), pp. 135-136.

feel himself respected for his work and diligence in providing for his family.

Appreciation shown by small gestures and words

Small acts and words of appreciation, naturally and sincerely given, are very important in the daily routine of living.

A wife feels appreciated and admired by a simple compliment: "That dress looks very elegant on you. Is it new?" Or "How nice the table looks today. The flower arrangement is lovely." Or "That was a magnificent meal? Where did you find the recipe for that roast pork?"

A word of praise about the hobby of the husband would likewise be well received. "The new fertilizer you added to the flower bed works wonders. It is because of you that the flowers in the arrangement are so luxuriant." Or "The trout we are having tonight is compliments of a certain good fisherman I know! I can't believe the size!"

These small comments and gestures create an atmosphere of cordiality that makes life genial for the wife and the husband, as well as for the children and relatives who observe it. Customary courtesies extended on a daily basis – the unfailing "please" and "thank-you," the simple compliments and acknowledgements of small kindnesses offered – are signs of the respect and admiration that each one has for the other. Furthermore, this example has a communicative quality: It will transmit a refined spirit to the children and to all who enter the house.

Unless mutual consideration exists, a disharmony comes into the picture. Once some friends were visiting the home of a couple who had recently remodeled their living room. The wife was showing the room, taking credit for all the improvements – the inlaid wood floor, the crown molding, the new drapes and upholstery.

After her lengthy presentation, the husband remarke in passing, "Oh, I thought I had something to do with designing and laying the wood floor..."

He was clearly aware that his wife was taking all the credit to satisfy her desire to be the center of admiration. Can you imagine this couple later, after the guests have departed? Even if the husband does not complain, he may well harbor resentments that will surface later. In any case, his esteem and admiration for his wife has been diminished.

When incidents like this occur often, it is inevitable that a certain distance will begin to appear in the couple's relationship.

Do not take credit for everything, even if you did the lion's share of the work. If it is appropriate, share the merit of a work with your spouse. How quietly pleased a wife is when someone praises her husband for their well-landscaped yard, and he does not hesitate to respond, "Thank you. But the credit for the flowers goes to Betty and her green thumb."

Or when someone praises the wife's apple pie, you can understand her husband's pleasure when she amiably replies, "Thank you. I'm glad you like it. I think a pie is always better when you have homegrown apples, and, thanks to Bill, we had a wonderful harvest of apples this year for my pies."

Queen Elizabeth II would have sufficient reason to assume the first place in decision-making, since she is the Queen of England and her husband is only the Duke of Edinburgh. When she announces a decision in public or in private, however, she always says, "My husband and I have decided ..." It is a good example to keep in mind of a consideration designed to maintain harmony.

Dealing with the other's defects

One of the most important points in nourishing a good relationship between a couple is for each one to show understanding for the shortcomings and imperfections of the other. In the routine familiar life of a couple, the day inevitably arrives when one party becomes acutely aware of the deficiencies of the other. How he or she reacts to that revelation is very important for the harmony of the marriage.

The understanding of defects that we are talking about here does not result in a "live and let live" attitude: "You can have your shortcomings, and I'll keep mine." A complacent or accommodating spirit is not the fruit of an authentic mutual respect. The correct position is to understand the other's defect and to amiably help him or her to correct it. The good spouse tries to understand the other and never ceases trying to gently correct his or her faults.

For example, Mr. Brown has lots of energy and is very disciplined – traits that make him quite capable of organizing and running a business. He wrongly assumes that everyone has his same energy level and, therefore, a self-discipline equal to his. Such a person normally becomes irritated with anyone who does not follow his model. Because of his lack of discernment, he runs the risk of brutalizing his relationship with his wife and children, and even with relatives and friends.

The wife of such a man needs to understand his shortcomings. She should help him little by little to see that others are different from him. Using tact and consideration – the very qualities so lacking in his behavior – she can help him to realize that his position is not appreciated by his family members or acquaintances, and can actually do them harm. To conquer such a psychology can be the work of years, or even a lifetime. Nevertheless, the solution remains the same – great patience and constancy on the part of the spouse.

The husband should also help correct the shortcomings of his wife. Mrs. McNeill has the defect of talking too much. She needs to communicate in order to satisfy her naturally expansive personality. This is understandable and can even be appealing at times. But if she never allows her husband sufficient opportunity to say what he thinks, her constant talking will become disagreeable to him.

An uncontrolled loquacity generally annoys others as well, and, if she insists on refusing to give others the opportunity to talk, she will soon find herself with fewer and fewer friends who will listen to her.

Her husband, without delivering stern sermons or making sarcastic remarks, can gently help her to see that in a social circle everyone is supposed to have an opportunity to listen and to speak, thereby facilitating a conversation rather than a personal exposition. If she is open to understanding the problem, she is already one step down the road to correction.

What is certain is that in any marriage the defects of the respective spouses begin to appear. He is disordered and never puts anything back in place; she has the habit of exaggeration; he laughs too loudly; she slouches and walks pigeon-toed, etc. It is also certain that these shortcomings will begin to damage the couple's good relationship unless they are dealt with properly.

Everyone wants to be respected for his or her positive qualities, but in a good marriage the spouses should also feel that their defects are understood and are being gently guided toward correction. Each one should courteously strive to bring the other to a better position, with the high aim of fostering harmony and virtue in the family. In this way, the spouses act toward each other as God acts toward them.

Confidence demands loyalty

It is to be hoped that in marriage a man and a woman can communicate freely and confide in one another. The quickest way to lose such confidence is to reveal private communications to others.

A husband who learns his wife broke his confidence and told her mother or sister a private matter about his work will no longer trust her with any information about his business affairs. A wife who discovers her husband told his friend about a private argument between the couple will feel angry and betrayed. For either party to mention private affairs to others – even another family member – is an inviolable breach of confidence.

Loyalty, one of the courtly qualities in the chivalric code of honor, translates into several very simple rules in a marriage:

- Never reveal the confidences you receive from your spouse.
- Do not criticize the other to relatives or friends.
- Always present your spouse to others in a good light.
- Do not tell stories that, even indirectly, can humiliate your spouse.
- Defend each other against the criticisms of others.

To keep the trust of your spouse you should also observe these simple rules:

- Do not open each other's private mail.
- Do not listen to the telephone conversations of the other.
- Do not pry into the contents of his or her private desk, purse, briefcase, notebook, or e-mail.

The advice exchanged between conjugal partners should also be kept in confidence.

Prudence should always be present in counsels given by one spouse to another. Does your husband ask your advice on a particular topic? You would be prudent not to infer that he is giving you the liberty to make a general criticism. If you want him to pay attention to your counsels, remember to restrict your opinion to the topic addressed.

Also, it is a mistake to assume that one request for advice opens the door to that topic forever. "Well, you asked my opinion, so I'm giving it," is poorly received when the new piece of advice comes three months after it was requested. This is often a cause of misunderstandings. In matters of counsel, always wait to be asked. Then, after giving your advice, let the subject be closed.

If your wife asks advice, listen attentively and courteously to her explanation before offering any counsel. Often, if a lady is preoccupied with a situation, she forgets that you do not have the needed background or details about the case that she knows so well. Then you should be patient and try to discover the full picture by asking calm, polite questions that will assist you in offering help.

If you criticize her exposition, or simplify the problem and impose your opinion, she will soon judge you as a man who lacks understanding – a kind of dictator – and will hide her problems from you.

It is also a mistake to become impatient and lose control of your temper because of the insufficient data she provided. Soon you will find that she is seeking counsel elsewhere to avoid your bad moods.

The role of familiarity

A deep and reasonable mutual respect normally translates into a relationship that is simultaneously familiar and ceremonious.

Today familiarity is often falsely understood as the right to tease each other all the time. He makes a joke or comic remark about her hair; she replies with a sarcastic observation about his receding hairline; the ball bounces from one court to the other. This spirit of constant mockery is a false conception of familiarity that has a very dangerous consequence: It has an innate capacity to destroy. Such bantering matches sooner or later end with hurt feelings and repressed anger.

For this reason, courtesy sternly commands that no one should ever be ridiculed. It warns that the constant joker is no different from a clown. At heart, every man or woman wants to be taken seriously, especially by his or her spouse.

Another false notion of familiarity is that it permits one to share prosaic things. Vulgarities and foolish banalities should always be avoided. They invariably lower the respect of one party for the other. They also indicate a lack of consideration for oneself.

A Catholic, conscious of his dignity as a son of God, never loses sight of that dignity. The Catholic lady and gentleman understand that the ideal of perfection should be sought not just in the spiritual sphere, but in every aspect of life. With this high goal ever in mind, the couple that strives for perfection makes every effort to avoid sharing prosaic actions in day-to-day life.

Here are some simple, small ways to show your respect for each other:

• Close the door of the bathroom when you are using it, even when only your spouse is at home.

• Be sure that your common bathroom is aired and clean before you leave it.

• Use a deodorant – more than once a day if it is very hot and you are doing heavy work that makes you perspire.

• When you change clothing or undress, do not leave your soiled clothing around for your spouse to see.

• Do not walk around in your underwear in front of your spouse.

• Do not bite or trim your fingernails in front of your spouse or leave the clippings on the floor.

• Do not brush your teeth or use dental floss in the presence of your spouse.

In our opinion, a general indicator of culture and a courtesy for your spouse is the habit of taking a daily shower or bath. Cleanliness of body and a pleasant fragrance are companions of courtesy.

Actions that are censurable in public should also be avoided in the couple's home life, such as cleaning the mouth with the finger, licking the fingers, picking the teeth, belching or expelling gas, yawning or coughing without covering the mouth, scratching the body, or spitting in the presence of your spouse.

These simple rules were once considered elementary laws of courtesy and were not considered necessary to mention in a manual. Today, however, they are constantly violated in the name of being spontaneous, natural, or humorous.

Nonetheless, such actions are often irritating and revolting. We are sure that if spouses were considerate of one another and avoided these small vulgarities in each other's presence, the general tone of the household would be more civilized, and the husband and wife would enjoy a mutual respect. The children would naturally follow their good example.

An upright familiarity in marriage depends upon factors rarely considered today: a good dose of self-discipline, a strict regard for the feelings of one another, and a careful observance of the proprieties of decent living. Such behavior is the opposite of the indolent self-indulgence, flippant spirit, and careless informality of the modern way of being.

Ceremony, a requirement for harmony

Anyone who proposes to live with another in a civilized way will find it most useful to maintain a certain ceremony in living.

What is meant by ceremony?

Ceremony in daily living first requires a respect for the differences between spouses. From this, a normal formality in speech, manners, and treatment of each other will follow.

The husband and wife are two separate, different persons. One day each will have to answer for his or her own life before God. Both have their own personalities, temperaments, and ways of being. Even after they are married, they need to have the privacy to develop themselves. It is a requirement of seriousness.

One simple way to respect the privacy of your spouse is to allow him or her to have certain times of silence. Silence often is more valuable than conversation. "Speak, if you have something more interesting to say than what the silence tells me," was a wise axiom of the older generations in Europe.

Does he like to read? Respect his silence, allow him time to be with his books. On Sunday morning, make sure that he has some time to read the newspaper. Arrange his chair in the study, set out a cool drink or hot tea, instruct the children not to bother him, and leave him alone. He will appreciate this consideration and be grateful for your understanding.

Is she a little romantic, somewhat melancholy? Did you try to tell her something, but she was distracted and didn't hear you? Leave her alone to paint a watercolor, weed the garden, or prepare a new dish in the kitchen. Buy her a new paint palette or interesting cookbook to show that you understand her need to be alone. She will be grateful for such consideration.

No one wants to talk and be together day in and day out. We need a certain time for recollection in order to be ourselves. In fact, that time to ourselves allows us to be more genial and interesting when we converse. An intelligent maxim states, "Two days without reading, banal conversation." We would translate it more broadly: "Two days without any time for recollection makes for dull companionship."

Nothing is more disappointing than empty, boring prattle and talk. Interesting talk, strangely enough, is born from silence and solitude, from reading books, leafing through art or photo albums, or listening to elevating music.

Great peoples produced high, charming cultures because even the simple classes loved to talk about art, music, and cultural things. Their conversations were not limited to the practical matters of work or technical details. Such things were dealt with at their proper moment, but they did not dominate a person's private time and conversation.

What we are suggesting is this: *First*, you need to allow times of silence and recollection for yourself and your spouse. *Second*, you should try to become more recollected, to take the time to develop yourself and to gather and order your thoughts so that you can share them later with your spouse and others. This will improve the general conversation in the home and raise the cultural level of the family.

Just a word in passing: Please, turn off the television, radio, computer, and electronic devices that are so omnipresent today. No privacy, recollection, culture, or civilization is possible with constant television and internet. If these machines take up every moment of your spare time, you may, indeed, follow the most recent news, stay abreast of the latest fads and fashions, and keep up with new music hits and releases. You will never, however, be a civilized gentleman or a refined lady.

If you respect the times of silence and privacy of your spouse, you are prepared for the next step in ceremonious living – the dignified and respectful treatment of one another.

How you speak to your spouse is an important way to show your consideration. As much as possible, be more formal, less casual – and never vulgar.

For example, when he is reading his newspaper, don't interrupt him by shouting from the kitchen: "Time to eat! If you don't come right away, the food will be cold!" Take the extra steps to stand in the doorway of the living room and say: "Mark, lunch is served. It's ready as soon as you can come to the table."

You delivered the same message in both cases. In the first, however, you appealed to his animal nature, calling him to the table like a master calls a dog to eat. In the second case, you appealed to his spiritual side and made him feel your consideration for him and desire to please him. Which of the two styles is more beneficial for the couple's life? The second, the ceremonious way, of course.

When she is paging through a photo-album waiting for you to pick her up, do not honk your horn and yell out the car window: "I'm here! I'm running late! Hurry up or we won't make it!" Stop the car, enter the house, find her, and calmly say: "Susan, my dear, I'm sorry I'm late for our lunch with John. Should we call him to let him know of our delay or just go ahead and try to make it anyway?"

Again, the message is the same. The first method produces a nervous woman who enters the car in a bad mood, blaming you for the delay. Unconsciously she is reacting for being treated like an animal or a piece of luggage you stopped to pick up. In the second case, you treated her like a dignified person, your companion for life, your wife. She feels the difference.

The drive is calm, the good rapport of the couple improves. The two arrive at the luncheon and spread the harmony that they enjoy between themselves.

Ceremony calls for good manners

It is clear that ceremonious living requires a constant attention to the laws of courtesy. The routinely executed small courtesies of daily living result in harmonious relationships and a cultured home life. We sincerely believe that many divorces and separations could be avoided today if men and women followed the more formal and ceremonious manners of the past.

For the husband's convenience, we will list a few of the elementary rules of courtesy that he should practice in the home:

• At a doorway, let your wife cross first.

• Open the car door for your wife both when she gets in and gets out. Yes, it involves extra time and effort, but you should make this small courtesy a habit. She will feel dignified and respected and will return the consideration in many ways. Your life as a couple will improve.

• At the dinner table, seat your wife, standing behind her chair and pulling it out slightly for her to sit down. This example will have a good effect on your sons, who will admire the respect you show for their mother and emulate your gentlemanly manners.

• Bring your wife flowers from time to time, even if it is not a special occasion.

Are you walking together on a sidewalk?

• Offer her your arm for support.

• Always take the side closer to the road, and leave the inside for your wife. It is a courteous way to show that you are protecting her from the danger that can come from the street.

• If a drunk or suspicious-looking man approaches when you are walking with your wife, put yourself between them to protect her from any possible embarrassment.

In turn, the lady of the house may repay the protection her husband gave her in public with her own gestures of consideration inside the home. We offer a few examples here:

• Treat him as the head of the family, showing him respect and offering small courtesies to show your attention and deference.

• Keep his study or office clean, air the room to keep it fresh, and periodically wax the floor or leather chairs.

• On Sunday morning make the waffles or blueberry muffins that he likes for breakfast. During the week, when he arrives home from work, have a good dinner prepared for him, perhaps with a preferred wine or special dish you know he likes.

• Wait for him so that you can eat together, making light conversation in an atmosphere of simple formality.

• Serve the dinner at a properly set table, covered with a clean tablecloth with his napkin is in his special napkin ring at the side of his plate. See that the glasses are clean and sparkling, the silverware correctly placed.

• Serve the water from a pitcher, not a plastic bottle that comes straight from the refrigerator. Serve soda or beer in glasses, never straight from the cans.

• Bring the food to the table in an appropriate tray or plate, not in pots and pans from the stove.

He will appreciate your effort to surround him with ceremony at home, just as you appreciate his effort to treat you well in public.

Be ceremonious. We realize it is a difficult order for today's modern couple. It requires a decision to assume a different way of being, to abandon lazy and casual ways that can offend or demean, and to make consideration for your spouse a first priority. When ceremony becomes habitual in a home, a natural harmony ensues. Contrary to common thinking, the fruit of ceremony is not severity or stiffness. Rather, it is harmony and sweetness of life.

Be ceremonious, and both of you will realize the great consideration you have for one another.

* * *

Chapter IV

The Father and His Children

The home is the child's first and most important school of courtesy. Parents who establish correct relationships with their offspring reap the good harvest of children who are obedient, respectful, and happy their entire lives.

Such fortunate children appear to acquire good manners and consideration for others naturally, but, in fact, they assimilate this conduct from their parents and are just reflecting, like small mirrors, what they see and experience at home. A boy can only behave like a gentleman if he sees one in action. A girl will be feminine and gentle if she admires and copies a mother's gracious manners.

There are a few general rules, formerly practiced instinctively in Catholic families, for establishing a correct balance of affection and firmness in the relations between parents and children. A father should exercise more firmness with his son so that the boy will become a man and learn to control his bad inclinations, assume responsibilities, develop perseverance, resolve problems, and have a strong sense of honor and duty.

At the same time, a father should show more tenderness and affection with his daughter in order to make her feel protected and loved. This behavior also instills in her a profound self-respect and sense of security.

A mother, on the other hand, should exercise more affection with her son, winning him with her goodness and piety and inspiring in him a great consideration and respect for women. This behavior will foster his natural tendency to protect and defend ladies in all circumstances of life.

With her daughter, a mother should exercise more firmness so that the girl will not be lazy, vain, or self-centered, but capable of the generosity and self-sacrifice that life demands. A mother needs to prepare her daughter to face life with dignity and a noble spirit and to realize that it is never without trials, disappointments, and sufferings – not an imaginary dream of romance and endless pleasures.

This harmony in the roles of the parents follows the natural order of things in a family. The role of the father beautifully balances that of the mother.

Parents used to know how to balance their authority with goodness and their affection with firmness. One generation learned from another. Less than a century ago no one needed to tell a sheep farmer in the Asturias, a shopkeeper in Alsace, or a tobacco farmer in Virginia how to exercise authority in his home. Each did so naturally. Their wives, embodying the spirit and particular charm of their regions, knew how to give their children warmth and affection, even while exercising a firm hand that put up with no nonsense or disobedience.

Both father and mother received this ability as a legacy from their own parents. This is tradition in its first meaning, from the Latin verb *tradere* – to hand over, deliver, bequeath. One generation handed over its customs and way of life – its traditions – to the next.

Past generations had an advantage that modern parents lack. Reared in a society that still had a sense of hierarchy, they had an innate understanding of their God-given right of parental authority in the family. They were not filled with uncertainties or confused by new theories of child-rearing "experts" preaching permissiveness.

According to these "experts," spanking teaches violence; rules and discipline stifle creativity; every command requires an explanation. Such theories left parents insecure and caused them to deny almost nothing to their children. This teaching is strongly influenced by neo-pagan psychoanalysis, which is opposed to the 2,000-year-old Catholic pedagogy.

Unfortunately, after Vatican II the Church began to adapt to the modern world, paying respect to those deleterious modern theories. We believe that, without this change, the modern child-rearing theories would have been wiped from the slate by now as anti-natural and harmful for the formation of children!

Catholic parents used to understand that, when they brought a new life into the world, they were responsible for not only the physical well-being of those small persons, but also their moral formation. They knew that, without discipline as well as love, it would be impossible to educate children stained with original sin.

Their attitude in face of this task was serious, a gravity that was reflected in their demeanor, way of dressing, and way of being. Their expectations were high, and children rose to meet them. Consider how a family portrayed itself in photographs and pictures in days past: the children were well-dressed, carrying themselves with the dignity and self-restraint they saw in the adults around them. The plenitude of the adult age was their model.

Contrast this with the portrayal of families in advertisements and on television programs today. We find a diametrically opposed relationship: the adults are dressed and acting like children. They mimic teen jargon and mannerisms to appear young and silly. It is difficult for the children of such parents to find mature role models and to face life seriously.

A father, not a buddy

St. Francis de Sales noted that the affection borne by fathers to their children is not called friendship, because friendship assumes a certain equality in vocation, rank, or aims. This equality does not exist in the affection of fathers for their children. The love of fathers, he says, is a majestic love, and that of children is a love of respect and submission.

A primary Catholic rule, then, for establishing a correct relationship of a father with his sons and daughters is that the father must be aware of this difference and must exercise his role in a serious and consistent way.

Fearful of appearing authoritative or aloof, many young fathers try to be "good buddies" to their sons and daughters, playing, joking, and making life a game. By doing so, they teach their children not only that life is not serious, but that authority is frivolous.

Instead of showing the stability that a child needs to be calm and secure, today's modern father takes on the air of a big child – dressing, speaking, and acting like a child. Everything is a joke; he is the clown who makes everyone laugh. The father is the Big Boy; his son is the Little Boy. The almost inevitable consequence is that his wife, the only one who keeps a certain distance, takes on the role of mother to both.

We observe this disorder everywhere around us. Take, as an example, the television commercial where the mother arrives home from shopping. She is putting away groceries and talking to her husband and children, who are sneaking the snack packs out of the shopping bad and eating them behind her back. At a certain point, she begins to look for the snack packs and cannot find them.

She is only momentarily confused. Looking at the guilty faces of her husband and children, she realizes they have eaten all the treats. She wags her finger at them and says, "Oh, you guys!" as if to say, "Naughty children! You are impossible!" Her children and husband grin and look at each other sheepishly, as if to say, "Well, what did you expect from us?"

In a scene like this, apparently very harmless and good-humored, there is an inherent disorder. The wife, who should be under the authority of her husband, has to assume the role of the only responsible adult in the family. The children begin to think they are equal to the father and lose respect for him. The family balance is upset because paternal authority is lacking.

The results of this syndrome are disastrous. Sons, as they become young adults, will seek their role models elsewhere. Later, they will resent the fact that it was the mother who exercised the primary role of disciplinarian. This resentment can affect their attitude toward women. Daughters will think that all men are big boys to be harnessed and disciplined by women. Later, following the example they saw as children, they will readily wield the primary authority in their own families.

We know that this is a very difficult thing for the modern man to face, but what is required is a change. Put away your shorts and sandals – don't dress like a boy. Stop the constant joking – be serious with your sons. Don't use vulgar language, slang and jargon – speak with the dignity befitting a Catholic father. In short, to paraphrase Scripture, put away the things of a child, and *esto vir* – be a man.

You will be surprised at the positive change that will naturally follow in your relationships with your children and your home life in general. Not only your sons and daughters, but also your wife, will show you more respect and acknowledge your authority. You will be setting the tone for the family – what you are called to do – and they will instinctively follow your lead.

The father and his son

How can a father establish the proper tone with his son?

If the father is serious and aware of the difference between his son and himself, the son's respect comes naturally. There is no need to give rules for that. The males in animal species treat their male offspring with a certain distance and are feared by them. Something similar takes place with human beings. If the father is serious, normally the son will have a healthy fear of him. The correct position for the father is not to eradicate the fear of his son but, rather, to transform it into respect for him and for what he teaches. It can be a powerful element to assist in the son's good formation.

If he wants to be obeyed, the father must show that he is accessible and must treat the boy with consideration. In times past, when men were very manly, the Church used to advise the father to balance his gravity with a kind and affectionate treatment of his son. Today, when men are frequently childish, it seems that the opposite advice should be offered: Balance your warmth with a certain reserve and distance.

In any case, try to keep a balance between seriousness and authority on one hand and accessibility and affection for your son on the other. To keep this balance is an important rule for the general formation of your son and for the particular topic of courtesy.

Signs of respect

Courtesy calls for your son to respect you and, consequently, to treat you with due honor. We have already mentioned the importance for a father to dress in a serious, mature way. It is not, however, only dress and manners that have become vulgar and egalitarian, but also speech. If you want to have a correct relationship with your son, you should make an effort to employ a more serious and formal language in your daily communications.

We realize that when we say "formal," many Americans instinctively cringe. It is because of the great American myth – a profoundly un-Catholic one – that everything formal is restrictive, artificial and offensive. Most of us have been formed since youth in the school of relaxed and casual language – not a praiseworthy institution. As proof, we offer the noxious results we see everywhere around us.

What we are suggesting is that you avoid using vulgar, common language and half sentences with your son. Don't use expressions like: "Get a move on!" "Shut your mouth!" "Hey, buddy, give me five!" Issue commands briefly but firmly, in full sentences: "Mark, remove your feet from that end table." "James, would you please bring me the hammer from the garage?" Your example is the first and best insurance that your son will be courteous.

From a young age, train your son to respond in full sentences. "Yeah," "Naw," and grunts are not acceptable. It should be: "Yes, sir" and "No, sir." A boy should frame his requests respectfully and formally. Instead of the insistent: "Dad, can I go, can I go?" it should be: "Father, may I have your permission to spend the weekend at Grandmother's house?"

The affectionate terms of "dad" and "mom" are certainly legitimate for small children still learning to speak. When used by older children or adults, however, we propose that they be used only in familiar conversations between the child and the parent. In normal conversations in the family, and especially in society, parents should be addressed or referred to with the more respectful "father" and "mother." The primitive "pop" and "ma" should be avoided, and the disrespectful "old man" and "old woman" prohibited.

If you want to set a good example of courtesy at home, please do not call your son "kid" when speaking or referring to him. Call him either "my son" or by his name: "How are you doing, Michael?" There is nothing wrong with using his family nickname on occasions: "Come with me, Mike; I know you will like what I have to show you." If he is a serious boy, he will be very pleased when you occasionally address him with affection and respect as "my dear Michael," or "my dear son."

Boys long to be treated with gravity by a serious father because this gives them a sense of their own dignity. Never dismiss your son with a joke or a laugh when he comes to you with an important concern. If you make a joke, he will feel that he is not understood, and the day will soon come when he will not return to ask your advice. This is one of the problems that often develop when joking has become the primary tone of a father-son relationship. It may seem funny and harmless at the time, but it has very profound and bitter consequences.

Give your son stability

You should be for your son what a harbor is for a ship. The ship is tied to the port in order to keep it from being washed out to sea. You should provide this same stability for your son.

A boy needs his father's protection – one that is not just financial and physical, but principally psychological. You should provide this protection with generosity and prudence. If a boy experiences stability while growing up, he will become psychologically healthy and able to calmly face the adversities of life while remaining faithful to his principles, for he has the foundation to be a principled man with a decided will. The unstable son – the boy without boundaries – can easily become a nervous man, probably an opportunist, a man without principles.

A great enemy of psychological stability for children is the television – even "good" programs without immorality. The constant shift of news, films, and commercials obliges the viewer to assume completely different states of mind in short periods of time, often only seconds. This onslaught destroys in the child's mind the possibility of any serious recollection or ordered attention. That is to say, it cripples the chance for your son to form the clear and coherent system of thinking necessary to orient his life. Frequent access to the television produces broken minds and slaves of the current fads – not men of convictions.

The television is also an enemy of courtesy. Even children's programs are littered with slang and bad words, complaisance with immoral situations, and the most vulgar and egalitarian ways of treating one another.

We have also noticed that on many programs it is the children who are presented as intelligent (often somewhat cynical in attitude), while the parents do ridiculous and foolish things. This kind of inverted presentation of the parent-child relationship will influence your child and work against the good authority you want to establish in your family.

Choose your son's companions

Another enemy of courtesy is bad company. Carefully choose your son's friends and companions. Do not believe the liberal myth that he must be in the street to know how to face life like a man. He will not conquer the street; rather, it will conquer him. Today the street is the Revolution in customs.

Respect for the marvelous

A father should respect his son's first period of life, when he is expected to have high dreams and marvelous ideas. The openness to the world of the marvelous is not a defect; it is the normal first approach of a child to life. He sees everything like a paradise. This is good. He is seeing the best side of reality, a side that reflects the perfection of God. You should (with prudence of course) allow your son to develop such a sense.

How can you accomplish this? A father destroys this innocence by laughing at his son's high aspirations or dreams. Even worse is the father who believes it is important for his son to put away idealism in order to be "practical" and prepared for the "business world."

If your son admires a beautiful beach, do not tell him, "This would be a good place to develop and build cottages to rent. Think of how much money we could make!" You may think you are very shrewd to instill a business sense in the boy. In fact, you are destroying in your son the sense of the marvelous and the ideal, and replacing it with an inferior way of viewing the world.

The role of sacrifice

For a boy to acquire the sense of sacrifice is very important. It is the father who plays an important role in helping his son to realize that suffering is a natural part of life and that he has to suffer to achieve what he wants in life.

The sense of sacrifice is what tempers the character of a boy. It also gives him the sense of reality, preventing him from being a "dreamer." We have seen men who are always planning some new grandiose scheme to make money or conquer the world, but they never accomplish anything. Usually they are defeated men. The best remedy against this disorder is suffering.

If you want a boy to be a man of strong will, a man of wise decisions, a man who understands his neighbor, teach him to accept suffering and to make sacrifices for the love of God, the Church, and his neighbor.

To make your son co-natural with suffering, do not hide the suffering of his neighbor. If someone in your family is sick, take your son with you on a sick call. Explain the illness and arrive at some good moral conclusion: "Yes, my son, it is hard to see Aunt Christine suffer like this, but think how difficult it is for her to be in bed all day in pain. Today it is her turn to suffer, but tomorrow it can be my turn, or your turn. The important thing is to be ready to bear that suffering well so we can face Our Lord at our judgment." Then observe his reactions.

If he becomes too fearful or nervous, calm him down, but return to the subject after a while. To be able to accept suffering is one of the most important sources of psychological balance and supernatural peace. To run from suffering and sorrow is, on the contrary, the cause of nervousness and affliction. Most of the nervous problems in adolescents and adults derive from this unwillingness to face suffering.

When your son hurts himself or catches a cold – or even a more serious illness – teach him to be conformed to the will of God and to offer his suffering to Him. Be kind and affectionate, but do not indulge or "baby" him, making him feel that he is the victim of some unreasonable fate.

Another important lesson a boy should be learning at a young age is to make small acts of charity. Let him help an elderly aunt with some yard work or carry her trash to the curb. Encourage him to make a small sacrifice by denying himself something he wants in order to give a gift to another less fortunate person of your family. At Sunday Mass give him some money to put in the collection to accustom him to the idea that we should provide for the Church.

A father should explain to his young son that it is normal for some persons to have more in life, and others less. Some persons lack material things, others are beggars in moral things, and yet others do not have the true Faith. Teach him to be grateful to Our Lord and Our Lady for being healthy and for having the material goods he needs. Most of all, stress how blessed he is to have the true Catholic Faith and to be in the state of grace.

A valuable lesson a father imparts to his son is to teach him to have recourse to Our Lord and Our Lady when he needs something. He should turn naturally to Our Lady in his troubles and triumphs and be aware of the presence of his Guardian Angel. He – like all the family members – should have his own small battalion of special Saints who are his intercessors in Heaven. It is the link between his family on earth and his larger one in Heaven.

This lesson helps to prepare a boy to face his future sufferings with courage, generosity, and gentility.

Instilling the spirit of fight

It is the spirit of militancy that gives the right tone to the spirit of sacrifice in the formation of a young man.

As we noted above, a boy should be conformed to suffer whatever is necessary for the love of a greater cause. But a father must teach him to analyze when and why he should bear sufferings. If, for example, the cause of his suffering is a bully on the playground, he should be taught to take a position against him and even be willing to fight if necessary. In all events, his aim should be to try to conquer the evil and, if possible, to turn it toward good.

What characterizes militancy is a willingness to face one's enemies and to counter-attack in order to win. A defeatist attitude does not belong to the Catholic spirit.

One way to form a boy with the characteristic of militancy is to present for his admiration the great heroes and saints that had this quality. Tell him, for instance, the story of Charlemagne and his twelve peers. Read to him the Song of Roland and comment on its deeds of chivalry. Teach him that the marvelous and good things he loves and admires need to be defended by him.

Hearing stories of the great deeds of heroes in armor, a boy dreams of fighting the enemies of the good cause, the cause of God. Give him a wood sword and shield. Let him begin his collection of toy soldiers and cannons. Such militant ideals should be supported and fostered, as long as they are not unreasonable. You will be providing him with horizons that will extend before him all his life.

The spirit of sacrifice and the spirit of fight are two invaluable gifts a father can instill in his son after the Catholic Faith. They will make a boy a virile, strong, and virtuous man – so rare in these corrupted, effeminate days.

Avoid the good life mentality

What a father should avoid at all costs is the formation of a son turned toward the good life. Unfortunately, today we live in a bourgeois society, a materialist world that despises nobility and adores comfort and self-gratification.

The noble mentality is directed toward the values we are stressing – the cross, sacrifice, effort, the fight, and re-building the kingdom of Christ. The bourgeois mentality is turned toward self-interest, the pleasure of the moment, making money, and having things. The noble spirit and the bourgeois spirit generate two completely opposite models of men. Unfortunately, a large majority of men in the United States are following the bourgeois model. It is why it has become so difficult to form a truly Catholic man.

If you want to form your son to be noble of spirit and truly militant, do whatever you can to prevent him from adopting the good life mentality – seeking the pleasures of life as his primary goal.

Here the father plays the most important role because the son looks to the father as his first model of what a man should be. If his father is only concerned with pleasure and obtaining new possessions – a luxury sports car, a new snowmobile, a big screen TV, the latest iPod – then the son will take his cue from him. Acquiring things while enjoying himself will be his primary aim in life.

If he sees his father as a man who places duty before pleasure, who takes his religion seriously, who leads the family in prayer, who becomes indignant at offenses against God and the Catholic Faith, who is willing to sacrifice and fight when necessary for a good cause, then he will realize that there are higher values in life than mere pleasure. And he will come to understand that not only is the noble path more worthwhile, but it is much more satisfying.

The sense of duty

The manners of the well-bred young man rely much less on rule books than on a strong sense of duty. To instill a sense of duty, the father must put discipline in his son's life. Duty and discipline walk hand-in-hand.

The best method to establish discipline in your son's behavior is to introduce him early to the sense of duty: "A man must do this." "A man does not do that." "God wants us to do this." This is a sure way for a father to form a man of character.

Among many other advantages, this discipline is the prerequisite to the introduction of courtesy and good manners. "My son, when adults are conversing, do not interrupt them. If you need to ask for something, you must ask permission to speak." "My son, a man never hits a lady. I never want to hear again that you hit your sister." He will follow your counsels because he wants to be like you and do things correctly, as they should be done.

Your son will always be checking to see if you also are fulfilling your duty, to see whether you practice what you preach. All children do this. They look for your good example.

You want him to be honorable and honest. But if you appropriate goods from your company, if you boast about cheating on taxes, if you laugh when you pocket an extra dollar at the checkout stand, or if you tell "white lies" in your day-to-day life, then you can be almost certain that your son will not develop standards of honor and honesty.

You would like him to learn the value of sacrifice, and so you ask him to renounce certain legitimate things from time to time. But, in order to truly understand the value and importance of sacrifice in daily life, your son must also see you curtailing your behavior and offering up lawful pleasures. Your example is very important in the formation of your son.

Treatment of women

As soon as a boy reaches the age where he can assert his personality, you should teach him to protect his mother and sisters. Again, this lesson is imparted much more by your example than your words.

If you argue with his mother in front of him or make sarcastic remarks about her, he will either revolt against you to defend her or assume similar bad attitudes with his sisters and, later, with his own wife. So, avoid these harmful attitudes.

If he sees you open the door for your wife, help her carry heavy items, seat her at the table, and show all the small courtesies a man should perform for his wife in daily life, he will understand the attitude he should have toward women.

Be objective and observant

In his relationship with his son, a father should be objective. He should observe the bad tendencies of his son at a very early age and begin to take steps to correct them. If he sees, for example, that his son has a tendency to laziness, he should first try to correct it in a positive way.

It does not benefit him to yell at him and call him names: "You are a lazy good-for-nothing and will never amount to anything." Rather, he should help his lazy son to undertake projects and complete them, and he should insist that the boy do his chores diligently. He must make sure that his son has a schedule and follows it.

But if the way of kindness does not bring the desired results, apply the counsel of Scripture, "He that spares the rod hates his son, but he that loves him corrects him betimes" (Prov 13:24). Indeed, the fear of God is the beginning of wisdom (1:7). How many persons are in Heaven because they feared Hell! So, do not hesitate to discipline your son so that he will be afraid to continue in his lazy ways.

If your son has a tendency to steal, to hit his sister, or to say bad words, punish him – sternly and firmly. You can correct the bad shape of a tree only when it is young and pliable.

The father of Gabriel Garcia Moreno noted that Gabriel had the tendency toward excessive fearfulness as a boy. He did not want his son to become a coward, so he would order the boy to enter a dark room and remain there for a short period in order to overcome his fear. This wise formation helped to make Garcia Moreno a very brave man who did not fear to face the Freemasonry of his day in defense of the Catholic cause. He became the exemplary Catholic president of Ecuador in the 19th century.

Observant fathers will find innumerable ways to counter the bad tendencies they see in their sons. We knew one father whose son was very good and pious, but with a tendency toward softness and timidity. He enrolled him in a self-defense class so that he could learn to defend himself and his principles. In a short time, the boy's self-confidence increased, and he had assumed a more manly way of being.

If you note that your son has a tendency to be silly or frivolous, take steps immediately to discourage such behavior. Remove the television, and avoid the friends who foster foolish behavior. Be serious with your son, telling him that God does not bless actions that are futile, frivolous, or impertinent. Young boys in their innocence are naturally serious. Sadly, it is often the parents' lack of seriousness and the family environment that make the boys flippant and silly.

Is your son self-centered and inordinately proud of everything he has and does? Do not allow him to brag. Show him in various ways how contemptible and ridiculous the braggart is in the eyes of others, and how false a position it is before God.

Does he lack the spirit of sacrifice? Help him to conquer himself by making small sacrifices, by not complaining if he is too hot or cold, by bearing the small trials of life without whining or avoiding them. Remind him that Our Lord told us, "If anyone will come after me, let him deny himself, and take up his cross, and follow me." (Matt. 16:24) If we want to be true warriors of Christ, if we want to do great deeds for Him and fulfill our vocation, we cannot be soft. We must take up the cross.

God gives parents the gift of discernment in these matters. It is not an infallible discernment, like the gift of the Holy Ghost reserved for Saints who are founders of Religious Orders. It is the natural discernment of parents in the state of grace who observe their children daily. If they have the eyes to see, they will note their children's bad tendencies in order to correct them and put them on the right path to Heaven.

The sense of honor

In our egalitarian society, each person is taught he must struggle to establish his identity and leave his own individual mark. In traditional hierarchical societies, a person derived his sense of self-worth by belonging to a certain family and class. It was not just money that determined a person's self-worth. It was his sense of belonging to an honorable family – in whatever place in society he was – and carrying on the family work and traditions.

The Catholic Church teaches that one should do his best at what he does, but the ultimate success is not a worldly one. Making money is not the end-all of life. A person who is good and practices and defends the Faith has a value and destiny that transcend any dollar value or career. A father should strive to instill in his sons this elevated mentality rather than the modern mindset, which so often results in nervous, dissatisfied, and unhappy men.

For the false modern model of success the only thing that really counts is achievement. To achieve, a man can do anything: cheat, lie, steal, or fool others. What matters is to win, regardless of how the victory is attained.

Following this wrong model, a construction worker advises his son at a young age that he must work hard to "make something of himself" in order to avoid being a manual worker like himself. The youth receives a double message: *First,* his father is of little worth because he does not have a prestigious job that pays lots of money; *Second,* he will be frustrated in life if he becomes "only" a good plumber or carpenter.

As we can see around us, this mentality leads to anxieties and stress. A person is never satisfied with his own place. Often his discontent makes him oblivious to the needs and feelings of others. Then he becomes rude – and can even glory in his rudeness.

Instead, a father who follows traditional ethics teaches his son that, while winning is important, he should always follow

Catholic Morals. If he loses after having done everything he could, he need not be ashamed. What is more important, he maintains his honor.

The most magnificent example of this honorable way to consider work is Saint Joseph, whose modest occupation as a carpenter is not highly rated by the modern mentality. However, God chose him to receive the two most honorable titles possible for a human being: foster father of Our Lord Jesus Christ and spouse of the Most Holy Virgin Mary.

The spiritual success of a man is incomparably more important than any business success. To be a faithful Catholic in the difficult times in which we live bestows on a man a great honor before God and man.

Be the spiritual head of the family

A father should play the leading role in the family with regard to the Catholic Faith. A son whose father does not lead family prayers, insist on the practice of virtue, or stress the importance of the Sacraments and Rosary will begin to think that religion is something secondary – a sentimental thing for women and old people.

At the same time, an exaggerated sentimentality in matters of religion can repel a boy and send him on a search to find a more virile model somewhere else. The firm, manly practice of religion, on the other hand, inspires devotion and respect.

The father and his daughter

A daughter needs much more affection from her father than a son does. For girls, feelings play a more important role than they do for boys. This is because girls express themselves through emotions, while boys express themselves through the words of a consistent language. God created them quite different.

So, you, the father, should take this fact into consideration in dealing with your daughter. When your daughter shows you tenderness, she is speaking her language. You should interpret it to understand what she wants to say.

She may be asking you for something without words, thanking you for a favor you did, or persuading you to do this or that. If you don't understand the message, she instinctively will either be frustrated with you or think that you are unwise. She is not expecting you to douse her with doses of feminine sweetness and tenderness; she is wanting you to understand her language and respond to her request.

You should show affection to her, of course, but don't try to imitate her tenderness. Show her affection according to your own manly way of being.

Much more than your son, she will notice when your affection is fake. The pat on the cheek or the abstract "What a wonderful little girl!" does not fool her. Neither does overly effusive praise and forced enthusiasm. Be authentic. Speak your own language. Show her a manly and serious affection. It is what she is expecting – and needing – to receive from you.

Your daughter will be very pleased when you treat her with a special solicitude and consideration. Present her with a bouquet of flowers for her birthday or on a special occasion when she made an effort and excelled. Ask her advice about small things, e.g., whether or not your tie matches your suit. You will see that she will return these small courtesies with admiration and respect for you.

Establish a stable and secure environment

The affection of a joking, childish father may amuse your daughter, but it does not inspire respect. One of the worst things for her formation is to have a "comedian" father. You may think that you are entertaining and impressing her. In fact, she will instinctively consider you a fool and look elsewhere to have her psychological needs met.

Even more than your son, your daughter needs your support. Since a girl was made to be a homemaker, she does not have the innate skills to face the world. She relies on you to protect her against the uncertainties coming from the outside world and the brutalities of her brothers and cousins coming from inside the home. Therefore, you should provide for her this security and protection.

Do not allow your sons to hit or punch their sisters: "John, stop that immediately. You know a man is never rough with a lady." Also, you should not roughhouse or wrestle with your daughter. It violates her feminine dignity and sense of security.

It harms your daughter to treat her like a son, taking her out hunting like a boy. Killing small game wounds the feminine spirit, so quick to sympathize with suffering and to protect life. There are different sports and occupations for girls. Rough games like soccer and football can injure not only the girl's more fragile body, but, more importantly, her psychology, encouraging her to assume rough, masculine mannerisms and attitudes.

It is very important to your daughter, like every woman, to have harmony and affection at home. She looks to you to provide this ambience much more than for your success in business or society.

A daughter is more susceptible than a son to insecurity, but when she has your support and senses your love and protection, she will feel psychologically stable and serene and will follow the good guidelines you give her. Since a daughter has a natural tendency to trust her father, you should take advantage of this trust to develop her feminine spirit and to guide her on the right path of good manners and high morals.

On the other hand, if she does not receive stability and courtesy from you in your relationship, after many disappointments she will push you aside and look for these qualities in an uncle, a teacher, or, more likely, a frustrated succession of boyfriends.

Consistent acts of courtesy

Whatever example the father sets regarding courtesy, the daughter has the natural tendency to follow it. If he treats her with delicacy, showing a respect for her femininity, she will be feminine. So many girls today have masculine tendencies and traits because they were not treated properly by their fathers.

What kind of courtesy should you show your daughter? A father may his thoughtfulness in many ways:

- Do not let her lift heavy objects or overexert herself.
- Do not use vulgar or coarse language, nor allow it to be used in her presence.
- Apply some of the courtesies you show toward your spouse to your daughter also. Note that we said "some of the courtesies" for an important reason. Some fathers may begin to treat their daughters with more consideration than they show their wives. This is a mistake because it upsets the order in the home. For example, the husband should always open the door for his wife and allow her to pass first. At times he may perform this courtesy for his daughter also when they are out.
- Respect her feminine instincts: her care for children and injured animals, her love for delicate and beautiful things. Never tease her for these natural tendencies, or she may react and assume a hardened, tough attitude because she thinks that this will win your respect.

If you do these things, the probability is great that she will obey your requests without the need for punishments.

Discipline

You want your daughter to obey you promtly. You are serious and respect her femininity. But it is also necessary for the father to demand that certain rules of good manners be followed.

This good conduct must be required on a daily basis in the home:

- An upright behavior at all times;
- Courteous conversation at the table and in the living room;
- No talking back or sarcastic remarks directed toward her mother;
- Absolutely no bad or vulgar language;
- No immorality in the home with regard to pictures, magazines, books, movies, internet, music, etc.;
- No immodest clothes, such as jeans, shorts or other men's clothing, mini-skirts, low-necked or revealing dresses, or blouses and skirts that are sheer or too tight.

Even though a daughter yearns for affection in her relationship with her father, she also needs firmness. She must learn that her father's word is the law of the house. Do not be afraid to exert your authority over your little girl, who actually desires an authority figure in her life. If you fail to do so when she is young, it will cause her great psychological damage later on.

Often the root of a father's hesitancy to discipline his daughter is the sentimental notion that he might hurt her feelings, causing her to love him less. In fact, the opposite is true. We once read an interesting study about rebellious teen-age girls in therapy. To the surprise of the psychologists, they found that these girls were rebelling against their fathers because they thought their excessive permissiveness was a sign of their lack of love and interest.

It is a curious paradox. The more lenient the father tries to be in order to please his daughter, the more critical she is of everything he does. On the contrary, the father who is firm and exerts his authority is deeply loved and admired by his daughter, who wants to please him and make him proud of her.

Chastity and morality

A father should always practice an upright and sincere conjugal chastity, and he should guard the honor and morality of the family. It is the father who must establish what he expects from his daughter in this regard, setting strict boundaries on what she cannot do because it offends God and dishonors the family name.

How false is the notion instilled in the American family that it is only the wife's role to be vigilant about fashions and the immodest clothing of daughters. "Why did you let her wear that?" the husband asks his wife. Or, worse yet, he assumes an indifferent attitude, leaving it up to his wife and daughters about what kind of standards they will follow in the matter of dress.

While the mother plays an important role by setting a good example in modest dress, it is the father, once again, who must be the authority figure and put a quick stop to wrongdoings. A strong word from the father to his young daughter will normally suffice to prevent immodest fashions from entering the house, when threats from the mother may have little effect.

One weekend we were visiting a family, and the ladies and girls were going out for a Saturday lunch. The father of the house was seeing us out. He took a look at his teen-age daughter, called her aside, and spoke quietly to her. She disappeared upstairs and returned in a different blouse – one that was not so tight-fitting.

Perhaps she might have argued if her mother had told her to change, but she did not question her father's command. She understood that he respected her and wanted her to respect herself.

Should your daughter take dance or gymnastics classes? This is not just a decision of the mother, who too often will follow the fashion set by her peers. Morals are more important than fashion, and the father must have a word to say in these matters.

A vigilant father does not want his daughter to become accustomed to wearing immodest clothing or displaying her body in inappropriate poses for the sake of athletics. Following good

Catholic Morals, he asks her to set aside gymnastics and certain sports, telling her that it is better to please Our Lord and Our Lady than the world.

By asking these small sacrifices of his daughter, the father teaches her generosity of spirit. And he does his daughter an incalculable service by helping to preserve her sense of modesty and her innocence.

Encourage your daughter's feminine spirit

We have mentioned this already, but it is a point of courtesy that bears repeating: Never treat your daughter like your son. It is a great mistake. How can her feminine spirit develop naturally if she is being asked to compete with her brother? Why should she make efforts to develop her domestic skills if the vocation of wife and mother is demeaned, while importance is given to a career and making money?

Women were made to rely on their fathers, brothers, and husbands. They were created to be the companions of men, not to replace men in their duties. A formation that emphasizes a career and salary causes confusion. If she follows this path, she will become something different from what her nature requires and will suffer the unfortunate consequences.

The modern independent woman is frustrated because men do not offer her protection or respect her femininity. She may respond by taking a negative or defiant position toward men. This attitude cannot bring her stability, peace, and happiness.

When you encourage these feminist tendencies, you effective destroy your daughter's future happiness. Instead of forming her to rear a family, help restore Christendom, and earn her crown in Heaven, you ruin her life by delivering her to the popular gods of modern Feminism.

One way a father can discourage this unnatural independence is to let his daughter know that she is expected to remain in the home until she is married. This used to be the tradition in Catholic countries in Europe and South America.

We knew a young woman from a good home in Argentina who was visiting a Catholic family in the United States. She was quite surprised to learn that the 18-year-old daughter was planning to move out and get an apartment the next year. "Why would she leave her home?" she asked with surprise. "Won't it be very difficult and lonely?" She was expressing the voice of good sense and Catholic tradition.

Let your daughter know from the time she is young that she is welcome in the home until she marries. If she does not marry, your home is where she belongs and is loved. She will be a treasure that you and your wife can count on until the end of your lives.

* * *

Chapter V

The Role of the Mother

It is always a pleasure to see Mrs. McGregor and her five children when they arrive Sunday morning for Mass at St. Patrick's. The well-dressed and self-confident children file quietly into the pew. The older ones help with 3-year-old Louis and baby Cecilia. Such discipline! Yet Mrs. McGregor hardly has the air of a drill sergeant.

Who can fail to notice the warmth and tenderness of this mother for her children? Each one basks in the warmth of her smile or tender word. The little ones delight to cuddle under her arm, like chicks under the wings of a mother hen; the older ones regard her with respect and affection. At the same time, if the boys become rambunctious or the girls begin to giggle, a stern look from her is enough to set them straight.

"How does she do it?" wonders Mrs. Parker from the back of the church with her two rambunctious young sons. How does she command such obedience and inspire such respect, while maintaining such an ambience of warmth and tenderness?

Many young mothers today are trying to find the proper balance of affection and discipline that emanates naturally from a well-established Catholic home. They want to be good mothers, but they feel lost and uncertain on an unknown terrain. Many did not have the example of a happy home life and were raised under the orientation of post-Vatican II priests and nuns who embraced the false premises of modern pedagogy.

According to this school of thought, one should allow the child to follow his instincts, without discipline or punishment. It is not surprising that, as a consequence, we have indexes of teen morality that are lower than those at any other period in History, higher rates of psychological imbalances among the young, as well as high suicide rates and increased criminality.

The salutary phenomenon of home-schooling is eloquent evidence that the post-Vatican II methods of instruction, implemented in Catholic schools for the last 40 years, have not worked. Unfortunately, these good-willed young mothers often have no defined direction to follow.

Permit us to give some simple guidelines, drawn from Catholic traditions and good sense, about how a mother can properly rear her children and establish correct relationships with them that will assure a courteous home and a happy life.

Tenderness and vigilance

Since the mother is the one who is with the children more often, especially in the formative years, it is very important that she develop proper relationships with them. It is principally the mother who contributes to the psychological well-being of her son or daughter, since the child's first contacts with reality generally occur through her.

If such contacts are in an improper or hostile environment, the child's psychological, moral, and intellectual development can easily be distorted or twisted from the very beginning. A child needs to be reared in a warm ambience of affection and seriousness, one that fosters healthy psychological growth.

God created women with a natural disposition to care for children. A woman's gifts – delicacy of sentiment and tact, charm, tenderness toward the weak, a readiness to sacrifice – make her admirably suited to be a mother. She should, therefore, use her gifts and instincts to train her children well.

The good mother intuitively understands that everything in the life of children is important because they are in the process of deciding the position they will take before God and before men. Children not only deserve, but also need, to be treated with respect. Nothing is more prejudicial for a child than to be regarded as a kind of toy or amusing plaything to make adults laugh. Today this treatment is very common, but it is harmful to the child and to the whole family.

The mother is called to create an atmosphere of affection around the child in order to foster the healthy development of his psychology. When a tree is young and tender, it needs to be particularly protected from adversities so that it can develop normally. Otherwise, it can be scarred or disfigured for life. Something similar happens with a child. When he is young and weak, he needs to be protected by an ambience of maternal affection until he has enough strength to face adversities. This protection is given by the mother.

She will be more determined to act this way if she realizes that the child will regard her affection and goodness as his first model of the love that Our Lady has for him. Her child's relationship with Our Lady is patterned in many ways on his early experience with his mother.

It is worth noting here that to protect the child in an ambience of tenderness does not imply that the mother should not give correction or discipline. If she has a false, sentimental notion of love and affection, she will not prepare the child for the sufferings of life that will inevitably come. If she over-shields her child and does not try to stimulate his courage, he will not be prepared for the fight.

The second piece of general advice we offer mothers is to be vigilant. Vigilance requires a mother to carefully observe the first reactions of her child to new situations and to direct him to foster his good side over the bad.

For example, she can observe her child's characteristics simply by watching how he acts with his toys. Is he an egoist, or does he have a naturally generous spirit? Is he more contemplative and abstract or practical and concrete? Is he withdrawn, or does he seek attention? Is hc timid with other children or a bully? Does he crave caresses, or is he more aloof? Is he content to be by himself, or does he love the company of others?

An observant mother will recognize her child's tendencies through a multitude of symptoms, and then she will stimulate his good inclinations and discourage the bad ones.

"To my mother, I owe everything," said St. Augustine. How many saints have said they received the foundation of sanctity from their mothers! On the other hand, how many bandits have blamed their scandalous lives on the bad example they received from their mothers!

An adult-centered home

Since this first premise – "Do not follow the school of modern parenting" – has already been determined, let us make a general observation, particularly pertinent for American mothers.

We have explained the myth of the Big Boy and how many fathers in our country do not exercise their proper authority at home, leaving the mothers to fill the resultant void. Instead of a Catholic patriarchate (the government of the family by the father), we find in most Americans families a matriarchate, where the woman commands. From this situation comes a lack of order and balance in the children and the home.

In a well-constituted family, the home life is centered on the life of the couple and their dealings with their relatives and friends. The children play a secondary role and are raised in parallel to this central family nucleus. The children are aware of such a difference, and, for this reason, they aspire to become mature in order to share more fully in the pleasure of the adult domestic society.

When the authority of the father is lacking, however, the mother instinctively treats both her offspring and her husband like children. The consequence is almost invariable: The house becomes a sort of kindergarten. Everything is centered on the children.

In this child-centered home, there is no privacy or ceremony. The living room, once well-arranged and suited for adult conversation and company, is transformed into a playroom filled with brightly-colored plastic toys. Dinner revolves around making sure that Junior eats his vegetables and does not spill his milk. When your brother and his wife visit, the conversation is disrupted by Angela's entrance, crying and screaming because her little brother overturned her dollhouse.

Do you plan to visit your friends? You have to warn them: "The children are coming…" This translates as: "Please, child-proof your house, and take any valuables out of the reach of my little angels, who want to feel at ease." After your visit, the lady of the house is obliged to clean spills on the carpet, remove shoe scuffs from the sofa, and deal with other similar disagreeable souvenirs. Your refined friend is hardly inclined to extend to you another invitation…

In times past, children would accompany their mother on social visits and would behave well. Of course, the mother's sharp eye was always watching to prevent unpleasant surprises, but there was no risk of a minor Vandal invasion. A mother prepared her children beforehand, telling them exactly what was expected of them: "When we arrive at the Johnson house, after greeting Mr. and Mrs. Johnson and the other adults present, I want you to go outside to play with the children. I don't want you to interrupt our conversation, except for something very important. If it is necessary to ask me for something, remember to say 'Excuse me' before you speak."

If John forgot and came inside to complain to his mother that he was hungry, he was kindly reminded by his mother: "John, I have a snack planned for later when we return home. I'm sure you are enjoying the beautiful day outdoors with your friends." He understood this coded message to mean, "If you continue this disruption, we will have things to talk about when we get home."

Today, little is demanded from children. They are the center of family life, and everything is adapted to their immediate needs and spontaneous demands. Many negative consequences result from this new school of thought.

Your children become accustomed to do whatever they want and do not understand the meaning of discipline or authority. They become self-centered, imagining that the whole world revolves around them. As they grow older, these bad tendencies can lead them into vices and immoralities that will have deleterious consequences until the end of their days.

Furthermore, this method of rearing children does not allow the mother a minute of privacy or rest, especially if she has many children. Although she believes that she is treating her children well by giving them her constant attention, she is actually forming them incorrectly and creating a kind of jail for herself. She cannot go anywhere or live at ease in her own home.

How can she resolve the problem? Here are some suggestions:

- Disregard the bad advice of the modern school of thought and manuals on child-rearing.

- Try to make your husband the center of the home. His needs and desires should be given first priority and placed above those of the children. If the mother takes this important step, the children also will respect his authority and view him as the head of the home, thereby enabling him to exert his proper authority.

- Make your relationships with your husband, relatives, and other adults the center of your family life. For example, children should not be allowed to interrupt adult conversation or to dominate dinner table conversation. When you entertain, the older children can be permitted to remain for a short time, but then they should be dismissed to engage quietly in their own activities so that the adults can converse at ease.

- Teach your children not to enter certain rooms in your home and not to touch the fragile and delicate objects that make up part of your décor. The house should not become one large playroom dominated by children's activities.

- Teach your children how to behave when someone visits your home or when they accompany you on your social visits. We know mothers who practice with their children what to say and do on a visit. There should be punishments for bad behavior, e.g., a privilege denied, a lost dessert, or the forfeited participation in the next visit.

- Do not make your outings and vacations child-centered. The aim of vacations and outings in times past was primarily to please and offer relaxation to the adults – not to constantly entertain and amuse the children, who were expected to behave well and enjoy the new sights and experiences.

In short, a consistent and wise discipline must be exercised in order to train your children to be polite and courteous. At first, this demands effort on your part; later the good results will be evident in the serene, well-ordered, and respectful environment that is enjoyed by the whole family.

A serious and genuine affection

The affection of a mother, as we said, is something every child needs for healthy psychological development. This is the primary duty of the mother.

But already here, in this first natural love a mother has for her child, there are some behaviors to avoid. We have seen many mothers who treat their babies like toys to show off to their friends: "Oh, look, isn't he cute?" "Did you see Bobby's expression? Bobby, make that face again. Ha, ha, ha."

This is not the right thing to do. Your baby is not your doll. He or she is an image of God, created to love and serve Him, and, afterward, to be with Him for all eternity. You have a very important role to play in helping him to reach this end. One of the first steps should be your refusal to view your offspring as an object of pleasure or self-satisfaction – an act of egoism that will ultimately be reflected in the thinking and behavior of your child. More precisely, you will spoil him from the beginning.

A mother's affection must be genuine. A child, who is much more perceptive than adults realize, recognizes when a mother's love is superficial or egoistic. The child may then make a decision to reject this fake affection and may resent the fact that his mother does not take him seriously. Behavioral problems usually follow. Or he may simply join this school of fooling others with fake sentiments.

The child needs a steady post – his mother – to assist him until he can support himself psychologically. What does a young child do, for example, who is being teased by his uncles in a family gathering? He runs to his mother. "Is that right, Mama? If I eat too many carrots, am I going to turn orange?" He is serious; he has a real concern – silly as it may seem – and turns to his mother for reassurance that this is a joke, that the reality is different. He wants his little world put aright again.

If the mother laughs at him: "You silly goose, don't you know anything?" he feels betrayed, thinking that his mother does not respect him. It is worse if the mother goes along with the joke, allowing her laughter to humiliate and bewilder him. If she engages in this behavior too many times, he will become confused and insecure, losing his trust and confidence in her. The child needs a serious affection from his mother.

Direct the tendencies toward the marvelous

One way a mother can nourish the good tendencies of a child is to direct them toward the sublime. The toys and gifts she purchases should stimulate in the child his sense of the marvelous, rather than the foolish, vulgar, or mundane. In this way, she prepares him to better understand the highest aspects of reality.

If your child is secure in his notion of what is good and beautiful, he will be able to recognize what is evil and ugly, and to make sound judgments on things. This ability gives the foundation for a calm and stable psychology.

Instead of stories about monster heroes, a mother should tell stories that teach the natural truths of the Catholic Faith, especially the epic deeds of the Saints and Catholic heroes from books like the *Golden Legend.* [6]

If her son likes stories of soldiers and battles, she should paint pictures with her words of noble and chivalrous knights who embark on great adventures and do good deeds. If her daughter likes stories of queens and princesses, she should recount tales of noble ladies with generous hearts who foil wicked plots. She should avoid stressing the romance in fairy tales: The emphasis should be on the good and evil that exist in this world and how the good must conquer the evil.

The medieval tales, so rich in teachings for children, should be selected carefully. The stories related to Charlemagne and his peers – Roland, Olivier, Guillaume, Archbishop Turpin, etc. – are splendid. The tales in the King Arthur series, however, have a distorted romanticism, conjugal infidelity, and a hint of the occult with the magician Merlin and the witch Morgana. A not-so-good secret society is set around the egalitarian Round Table.

It is good to be aware that, after the '60s, the hippy movement took over the medieval festivals and destroyed many laudable tendencies to rekindle interest in the Middle Ages through games and recreations. Nowadays, this hippy-medieval tendency has progressed to the point where it is common to see medieval knighthood presented with clear tones of the macabre, the monstrous, and even the satanic.

This trend was taken up by the toy industry, which has flooded the market with ogres, magic wands, and sorcery kits. Stay away from this kind of amusement. Do not buy monsters for your children. Select, instead, toys that reflect the truly marvelous and stimulate their love for God.

---

6. Jacques de Voragine, *The Golden Legend,* trans. by William Granger Ryan (Princeton University Press, 1995), 2 vols.

Seeing God in nature

A mother should also encourage her child to see the marvels in nature that God created for us in His great goodness. One does not need wealth or high academic degrees to teach children about God's attributes through observing His creation..

St. John Bosco relates how his peasant mother taught him to look up and gaze at the sky: "On serene and starlit nights, she took me outside and showed me the heavens and said to me, 'It is God who created the world and put so many beautiful stars above. If the sky is like this, how will Paradise be?'"

Simple lessons like this take deep root in the heart of a child.

Exercise your authority

To surround your child with an ambience of tenderness does not imply that you should withhold from him correction or discipline. The corrections you give have a double aim: to rectify a specific fault and to teach your child the sense of duty.

Because of an erroneous understanding of affection, many mothers do not punish their children when they disobey or misbehave. These ladies are filled with insecurities – the fear of being too severe, the fear that their children might dislike them if they do not give in to childish whims, the fear that they are fostering violence by punishing them.

Defects in a child sprout much earlier than many new mothers expect. We have heard mothers with unruly children explain that they will begin to discipline them after they reach the age of reason. That is much too late. Discipline needs to be applied as soon as the bad behavior appears. If you want to rear upright sons and principled daughters, you have to correct them from their earliest years.

When you correct your child, avoid a confrontation of wills, if at all possible. It is not good to issue commands by saying, "You have to do this because I say so." Naturally, when you give a command, your child should obey. But when he reaches age five or six, he may start to rebel against the continuous "Do this," questioning the reason for what may seem to him to be the purposeless idiosyncrasies of ladies.

It is nobler and more efficient to punish him by saying: "You should not do this, my son. It is wrong. This is the correct behavior." Then administer the punishment.

The first position puts the emphasis on doing what you want; the second puts the emphasis on serving an ideal. A child understands that his mother is not as upset with him as with the transgression of a rule that must be observed. There is a right way to behave in order to please Our Lord and Our Lady; on the contrary, there is a wrong way that displeases them.

You should serve the same ideal you are teaching him, that is, you should do things correctly. If you do so, he will implicitly understand that your position is one based on principles, and he will respect you. You have a much greater chance to form a superior adult with this second method than with the first.

How does a gentle mother fight her nature and sentiments to apply punishments? She is convinced she must do so for the good of her child. She wants her child to be courteous and upright, to love and serve God, and to detest what is sinful and evil. For this reason, she is determined to never let faults – not even small ones – go unpunished.

The more she consistently corrects her children in a calm and serious manner, the more they realize she does so because she detests what is wrong. Seeing her love for goodness and order, they will learn to love the same. Realizing her absolute repulsion for disorder and evil, they will learn to abhor it also. And they will regard her with respect and admire her goodness.

A mother should ask Our Lady to help her to balance her tenderness and love for her children with a consistent firmness and discipline. If she achieves this goal, she will have done her part in their good formation.

A consistent firmness

A mother has to be firm. Once she decides on the behavior she wants from her child, she should insist on it. If a child does not give prompt obedience, punish him. Do not make idle threats of future punishments, "I am going to tell your father."

Let us look at an example. Mrs. Jones takes her two daughters to the hospital to visit their aunt, and the amiable receptionist gives them each a trinket. Madeleine is only three, but she furiously insists on having the bracelet of her older sister. Her mother wavers. She is uncertain, afraid that Madeleine will throw a tantrum in public. After all, it is only a piece of junk jewelry.

"Okay, honey," she relents and instructs her elder daughter to give Madeleine her bracelet. "After all," she justifies to herself, "it is a very small matter." That is not the case. It is a large victory for the child. By giving in to her whim, Mrs. Jones stimulates her daughter's egoism.

The next day, Madeleine ferociously refuses to go to bed at her regular time. Her uncertain mother resolves the problem with a trick, "I'm going to read you one story – you get to choose the book – and then you have to go to bed." This does not teach obedience, nor does it trick our strong-willed Madeleine in the least. She accepts the deal and again claims the victory.

Bribery like this undermines authority and makes it more difficult for a child to develop self-restraint or self-discipline. A child should have a set hour for going to bed and should be held to it firmly. It is bedtime, and, without whining or begging for a few more minutes to stay up, she should put away her toys, take her bath, brush her teeth and hair, place her clothes in the closet or the hamper, and say her prayers.

Discipline on the part of the mother will give good fruit: children who will know how to face life and who will respect her.

If you need to ask the help of your husband to correct a child, do so, but not in front of the child or others, in order not to corrode your authority. Such discipline problems should be discussed with your husband in private.

Regarding discipline it is not superfluous to keep in mind these wise passages from Scripture:

- Whoever spares the rod hates his son, but he who loves him is diligent to discipline him. (Prov. 13:23)
- For the moment all discipline seems painful rather than pleasant, but later it yields the peaceful fruit of righteousness to those who have been trained by it. (Heb. 12:11)
- The rod and reproof give wisdom, but a child left to himself brings shame to his mother. (Prov. 29:15)

Mothers and sons

Because of the feminist myth that a woman can be like a man, the thoroughly modern mother has the idea that she can be a buddy to her son, another one of the "guys." This type of manly mother likes to joke with her son and his friends. She uses rough language and dresses like a man. No fancy table settings for her – she would rather be plain and practical like her boys.

This is not what a boy wants or needs. He wants a mother, not a buddy or scout leader. He wants to be taken seriously. He needs a model of feminine seriousness that, as a rule, translates into feminine courtesy. A feminine, courteous mother teaches him by contrast that he should reciprocate her courtesy and be a gentleman. Every mother should be a model of dignity in manners and courtesy for her son.

If the table is well set, the food attractively served, and the talk gentle and amiable, boys will soon realize that it is not clever or amusing to be boorish and rude during meals.

If a son is expected to address his mother with respect and open the door for her and his sisters, he will learn to treat all women with respect.

If he learns to respond politely to questions and is not permitted to say whatever he thinks, he begins to learn the art of conversation and how to please others.

If his mother is always appropriately and modestly dressed, he will understand that he should not appear in dirty or sloppy apparel before her.

On the contrary, if his mother barks out orders like a marine sergeant – "Get a move on!" "I said get out of bed now!" "I said shut up!"– he will assume he can respond in the same rough tone.

If his mother is sloppily dressed, wearing only what is comfortable and easy, he will take for granted that comfort and convenience are more important than discipline and propriety.

If he is allowed to eat at the table in his pajamas, his head resting on one arm, his fork held improperly, he will not develop the natural confidence of a gentleman.

If he can dominate the conversation with his banter and crude remarks, he will despise protocol and prefer to do and say what he thinks at the moment, falsely imagining that this behavior makes him a very creative and brilliant man.

The rough mother produces a rough son who regards women as buddies. The refined mother rears a gentleman who treats women as ladies.

We knew one boy whose mother was quite ill. He was very young and would visit her every morning, never finding her uncombed or disheveled. She always greeted him warmly and amiably, with great natural courtesy. Later he remarked that this made a strong impression on him, and he could never think of her without respect for her goodness and self-discipline.

Guard against overindulgence

How can you guard against becoming overprotective or overindulgent in your relationship with your son? First, regarding his defects, you need to be objective. Because of a mother's affectionate and protective nature, it is her tendency to want to cover for the defects of her son by making excuses for him.

When James speaks rudely to Aunt Mary, his mother counters with an excuse: "He's so tired. After all, he went to bed too late last night and hasn't had a nap." "It's all right," she tells her husband when he expresses concern that Louis is sleeping every morning until noon. "You know how bad his asthma is. He can't be outside anyway, so he might as well sleep." When your husband or another authority corrects your son, do not make excuses for him, even if they are justified.

It is also important to refrain from trying to resolve all the problems of your son. This fault is very common among protective mothers today. Mothers may think that they are helping their sons, but they are effectively crippling them.

Daniel receives a detention for laughing in class, but he convinces his mother that it was his friend who made him laugh. Poor Daniel! She rushes to take his part, makes an appointment with the teacher, and insists the punishment be revoked so that justice is done and her dear Danny can be spared this humiliation.

In fact, she has done a great harm to her son. It would have been far better for him to be punished by the teacher, even if the correction was too severe.

If you try to arrange each detail of your son's life with painstaking zeal, covering for his mistakes and defects, your attitude will undermine his spirit of initiative and destroy his capacity to resolve problems. He will not learn to make decisions or to face consequences. Instead of becoming a man capable of confronting difficult situations and bearing disappointments and defeats, he will remain a mama's boy who is dependent on you.

Ask your son to make sacrifices for you

It is difficult for a boy to develop consideration for women if his mother always does everything for him. Your son sees you sacrificing for him to make his life better and easier. Unless you ask him to make small sacrifices for you as well, he will become self-centered and egoistical, imagining that he deserves this constant service.

Try to arrange for him to perform services for you and to make this behavior automatic: "Oh, John, this package is heavy. Could you carry it for me?" "No, Mary, let your brother pick that up. After all, he's a man, and men don't let women lift heavy things." "Michael, I do not feel well today. I want you to play quietly for several hours while I rest a little. Please try to keep Bernadette from making too much noise. It makes me happy to know I have a responsible boy I can depend on."

You will find that your son will rise to meet your expectations and develop a generous and chivalrous spirit.

Avoid inordinate praise

When your son does the right thing, you should show satisfaction and pleasure, but not a disproportionate joy accompanied by high praises. He did what he should, so you should let him know you noticed that he fulfilled his duty. It is good, but not extraordinary. It is what was expected of him.

If you inordinately praise your son just for doing his duty, he will become self-centered and proud, thinking that he is accomplishing wonderful things when he is only doing what he should do. Then, if he does not receive this kind of praise from others (and in his adult life he most assuredly will not), he will become resentful and sullen, thinking he is not properly appreciated. Instead of a man to be counted on, he will become a big baby.

One of the worst things a mother can do is to instill in her son an exaggerated idea of his importance. Little Johnny is a boy of normal intelligence with an aptitude for music, but his mother is convinced he is a genius, another Mozart in the making. She hires the best teacher, buys a grand piano, and smothers him in praise and excessive attentiveness, giving him the impression that he is something very rare and extraordinary.

Her illusions of his grandeur will unduly flatter him today, but tomorrow he will have to face a harsh disappointment when he realizes his shortcomings. Even worse, he may continue in his illusions and suffer psychological problems as an adult.

If your son is intelligent, do not praise him for this attribute. There is no merit on his part in this blessing – it was a gift from God Who is the one to be praised.

His accomplishments should be modestly praised in matters that involve the will: He studies to earn a good grade, he practices a piece and performs it well. Also worthy of moderate praise are his good moral actions: He offers the best place to his brother, he refuses to lie, he averts his eyes from an impure picture.

If someone is more intelligent or talented than he, teach him to accept this difference with a good attitdue: "God gave Philip a great talent to play the piano. We should be happy for him."

If your son is not intelligent, do not try to fool yourself and him. If you do, you may hide this deficiency from him for a short time when he is young, but as he becomes older his limitation will become evident. The illusion you created will only harm and humiliate him.

Instead, take note of his lack of intelligence and discuss it with your spouse. By fostering illusions that your son will never be able to achieve, you help to make him frustrated or rebellious. You and your husband must prepare your son to face life by directing him toward an occupation where high intelligence is not needed and by teaching him to be satisfied with the talents God gave him.

We know some mothers who are always trying to convince others that their children are extraordinarily intelligent when they are not. It is apparent to everyone except the mothers. Mothers should try to be more objective. While they may, indeed, fool themselves, they are not fooling others.

Even if you imagine little Henry is a genius, don't broadcast the news. You will save your friends the bother of hearing your monotonous praise, and you will save your son from becoming the object of ridicule that follows this kind of exaggeration: "My goodness, can you believe what our brilliant Henry did today?"

Mothers and daughters

By nature, a girl will seek in her mother the model of what she should be. The instinctive movement of a girl's soul is to be enthused with her mother and to take her as a model. Therefore, a mother's role in the formation of a courteous daughter is crucial.

We have seen how a father should show more affection with daughters and more firmness with sons. A mother, however, must be willing to show more firmness with her daughters because she plays a larger role in their formation.

Understand your daughter

For a mother to have a good relationship with her daughter, she must understand her. Often a mother – especially an energetic, strong-willed woman – has the false presupposition that her daughter will be the mirror image of herself. While this is true in some cases, generally it is not. It is far better for a mother to regard her daughter as a soul very different from herself.

It is not difficult to find examples of mothers who misunderstand their daughters. Mrs. Sullivan has a very social nature. She enjoys luncheons and teas with her friends, shopping for clothing and items for her tastefully decorated house, chatting on the phone with her relatives and friends. She thinks and acts quickly, with a great deal of flexibility. Her daughter Mary Ann is quiet by nature, slow to make decisions, indifferent to fashions and shopping. She prefers to be alone, reading and daydreaming.

Mary Ann is an enigma to Mrs. Sullivan. How could this slow, languid child be hers? She labels her detached spirit as laziness and inability to focus. She cannot understand her daughter's lack of interest in shopping and outings and insists on her participation in order to improve her fashion taste and social skills.

Feeling inadequate and unable to meet her mother's expectations, Mary Ann withdraws further from her. Her relationship with her mother becomes increasingly strained, and she makes excuses to avoid the outings her mother enjoys so much.

"My mother doesn't understand me," she often thinks. As she grows older, she spends more time with her cousins at Aunt Joan's house, which is not as lovely and ordered as her own, but which provides a haven where she feels comfortable and accepted.

The mother and daughter are speaking different languages. What could Mrs. Sullivan do differently? She needs to make an effort to get out of her own world to understand her daughter. Then, instead of trying to change her daughter's way of being, she should help her to develop the good sides of her personality and to conquer her peculiarities. She should also gently help Mary Ann to correct her moral weaknesses and, with the help of grace, to overcome them.

"Tell me about the new book you are reading," Mrs. Sullivan might say to Mary Ann, encouraging her to express her thoughts. Above all, she must show a great patience in the face of Mary Ann's awkwardness and mistakes, enduring them without bursts of temper.

Without false presumptions, the wise mother seeks to discern the psychology of her daughter and to discover and encourage her genuinely good inclinations, while curbing the bad ones.

Fostering a spirit of generosity

For girls, it is most important for mothers to foster the spirit of generosity. Generosity is absolutely indispensable for the Catholic woman, a prerequisite to maintaining a good relationship with her parents, siblings, and relatives, as well as her future spouse and children. If she becomes selfish – like so many women today in the business world – she becomes despicable. Instead of being the light of the home, radiating goodness everywhere, she demands that the spotlight be directed on her. Nothing is more destructive for girls than having an egoistic mother.

The generous spirit – the willingness to give of herself and accommodate others, even at the cost of sacrificing her own wants and desires – is something natural to the woman. While a man naturally devotes himself to great causes and works, the woman by nature tends to devote herself to other people.

This does not mean she should be naïve, willing to do everything for everyone. She should dedicate herself to those who deserve her sacrifices and goodness – in this case, to her parents and siblings. And she should learn to make this dedication for a higher reason – not just to please others, but primarily to please Our Lord and Our Lady.

This generosity is something the Catholic Church understands very well. In her missionary work of the past, when she wanted to convert a people, she would send a religious order of nuns to that place to care for the sick or teach children. After those nuns had been in an area for a while, then the missionaries would arrive and start to preach the Good Word of Our Lord Jesus Christ. The missionaries knew how to benefit from the atmosphere created by the sisters' disinterested generosity, a charity only possible with the grace of God.

You want to inspire generosity in your daughters. To do so is impossible without a religious education, without love for God and Our Lady and the desire to sacrifice for them.

Let us offer this charming example: One of the daughters of the Marquise of Gramont asked for some water between meals one hot summer day. The Marquise kindly told her daughter: "My dear child, I am going to ask a small sacrifice of you. I want you to think of the thirst of Our Lord Jesus Christ on the Cross, and you will have the courage to wait until dinner."

This disinterested generosity is the antithesis of the spirit of advantage, which you should avoid at all costs. Unfortunately, this attitude is very common among some mothers: "Let's buy this fruit basket for Mr. Lewis because he has tickets to the carnival that he may give you." "Now remember to be very kind to Aunt Frances because she may leave you something in her will."

How do you form the spirit of authentic generosity in your daughters?

You do so by your example. Does your daughter see you willing to sacrifice, to set aside your wants in order to serve family and neighbor without complaining or murmuring? Does she see that you are willing to stand against the current fashion in your dress and customs in order to remain faithful to the principles of Catholic Morals? Does she see you praying, making every effort to go to Mass and receive the Sacraments of Penance and Holy Communion frequently? Are you fostering a strong devotion to Our Lady and the Child Jesus?

Mothers should avoid making critical comparisons: "Margaret has a pretty dress, but yours is prettier!" "You are the smartest girl in the class." Instead, they should encourage their daughters to admire the good in others. By doing so, they will help them to not become egoistical – imagining themselves to be the center of the world.

Another feminine tendency a mother should avoid is manipulation. Mrs. Williams asks her sister: "Patricia, could you please talk to Regina? Tell her she shouldn't be wearing that cowboy hat to Mass. She will listen if you say something because she likes you so much."

If a mother is manipulative, her children will soon realize it. It can harm their good relationship with her or, worse, teach them that this is how to act with others – even those closest to them.

Prepare your daughter for a work at home

Wrongly influenced by Feminism, some mothers instill conflicting notions that create confusion in their daughters' minds from an early age. On one hand, they teach their daughters to sew and cook and tell them that a woman's natural calling is to be a wife and mother. On the other hand, they encourage their daughters to pursue careers to become doctors or lawyers or other professionals, thereby pushing them into masculine roles.

Little comments like: "That was a good argument, Karen; you could be a good lawyer" or "You will always have a job if you learn to program computers" send the message to a daughter that she should have a career and life outside the home in order to be truly fulfilled.

A girl can easily resent this conflicting message because she innately understands how unfeasible it is to do both. If she does choose to pursue a career, she might later feel oppressed in it or have a feeling of emptiness and frustration because she neglected to fulfill her feminine vocation.

In the formation of her daughter, then, a mother should take particular care to lead her to that which makes her capable of fulfilling her duties as a wife, a mother, or a helpmate to her parents if she does not marry. Since her future realm of action is the Catholic home, help your daughter to learn the craft of housekeeping and to share in caring for her younger brothers and sisters. This is as important a part of her formation as her classroom studies.

The home is the natural place for daughters to learn and perfect concrete skills – cooking, cleaning, sewing, embroidery, art and crafts that beautify the home. Assigning daughters routine chores and jobs also provides an excellent schooling of the will. It forms the habit of decision, learned from the need to get through things that will not wait. Also, these domestic chores drive out silliness as effectively as the rod. They are a mighty weapon against sloth and pride, preparing a sane and balanced mind for the discipline of life.

A good mother knows this, and her relationship with her daughter is based in part on the concrete and practical knowledge of the skills of housewifery that she shares with her.

For example, the mother asks her daughter to set the table properly every evening – an exercise in aesthetics and discipline. "I know it is extra work," she explains as she arranges the food tastefully on a platter, "but everyone will enjoy the dinner more if it is presented well."

She knows how to encourage and compliment special accomplishments: "I believe that your apple pie is better than your grandmother's." "The flower arrangement you made is so lovely. I want to just sit a moment and enjoy looking at it." "Look how tiny your stitches have become! I'm proud of you."

If you emphasize those things that you learned from your mother, you may plant in her spirit the seed of a love for tradition: "This is my mother's special bread recipe." "This is how my mother taught me to fold napkins." "In our family, we always have Grandmother May's eggnog on Christmas day." The bond extends from one generation to another, binding the women together in a warm affinity and a sense of family.

If you want your daughter to have some means to help support her future family financially, there is work she can learn that can be done at home, without abandoning the care of children and house. Depending on her natural talents and interests, she can be encouraged to pursue sewing or cooking, to learn languages, to paint or practice the art of calligraphy, to play the piano or other musical instruments, to garden or arrange flowers. There are any number of such hobbies and skills that can be learned and practiced in the home.

A love for beauty and disgust for the vulgar

A girl is predisposed to love beautiful and elevated things. It falls to the mother to stimulate a taste for what is authentically beautiful and noble and to kindle an aversion for what is ugly and vulgar.

Sometimes a mother can misunderstand her daughter's love for beauty because of a false presupposition (inspired by Calvinism) which assumes that a girl who loves beautiful things – fine furniture, elegant clothing, refined jewelry, lovely silk and velvet materials – is necessarily worldly. This is not true.

A Catholic mother teaches her daughter to admire what is beautiful – to open her soul to the highest earthly values – in order to draw her to love and admire the splendor and perfection of God. Admiration for what is most elevated and refined is the foundation to inspire a true courtesy in girls.

Girls are extremely sensitive to their surroundings and external things. In their innocence they can be charmed and won by beauty and refinement. A wise mother understands this fact and fills her daughter's small world with delicate, charming, and exquisite things that will form her spirit to love what is good and beautiful.

She also trains her daughter to make good judgments and to discern authentic beauty from the fake: "Look, Maria, at this elegant plate. That blend of colors is so delicate, yet distinguished." "Did you notice the shape of that vase, Anne? It seems more refined that the one with the flat bottom."

Instead of many articles of cheap, faddish jewelry, a wise mother purchases a refined, tasteful piece of jewelry for her daughter's birthday – a pearl, which signifies purity, or a ruby, which symbolizes courage and sacrifice. Girls who appreciate beauty will also like to contemplate the symbolism of beautiful things. When this spirit is properly developed, they will seek these things not to possess them, but rather to admire them out of their longing for what is the quintessence of excellence – the perfection of God and the happiness of Heaven.

If, however, a mother is worldly, she will mislead these good predispositions of her daughter. Very soon her daughter will adopt the same worldly habits. She will learn a distorted vision of things, which affirms that beauty, refinement, and culture are desirable principally for the personal advantages they can give a person.

Cultivating refinement

There are many simple ways a mother can develop the spirit of refinement in her daughters:

• She keeps the house ordered and clean, the rooms arranged with beauty and charm. Good taste does not require great expense.

• She dresses in a feminine and dignified way. She does not neglect herself to the point where her daughter could be ashamed of her. If a daughter has the good example of a mother who never wears vulgar or immodest clothing, she will develop a natural sense of what is appropriate and modest.

• In her manners with her daughter, she sets the example by adopting a polite and dignified language. She says: "Would you please come here? I need your help with this." "Thank you for getting my scissors." "It's time for you to practice the piano. Please don't skip the pieces in your exercise book."

• She reminds her daughter to stand straight and sit and walk correctly: "Rose, please stand straight. Ladies don't slouch." "You know we don't sit on the floor like Indians, Elizabeth. Please get a chair and sit properly when you're playing a board game with your brother."

• In the same kind but firm manner, she asks her daughter to moderate her tone of voice (if it is too loud or strident) or to speak more distinctly and clearly (if she mumbles). She does not permit a whining tone or baby talk.

• She does not gossip about others in the presence of her daughters. A daughter who hears her mother criticizing others and discussing their faults can become an accomplished gossiper herself by the time she reaches her teens, preferring mean and petty conversation over lofty and elevated thoughts and considerations.

Curbing romanticism

It is very important to curb romanticism in your daughter at a young age. We are not speaking here of boyfriends *per se* but, rather, of the romantic vision of life.

Because the sensibilities of girls are much livelier than those of boys, girls have the tendency to yield to first impressions, to jump to conclusions impulsively. The unleashed imagination can very easily run away with them, and they can begin to imagine the world, the family, brothers, and friends to be different from what they are in reality.

Let your daughter begin to understand that this way of following impressions is wrong. Teach her to exercise vigilance over her first impressions and impulses.

Our approach is the very opposite of the school of modern child-rearing that instructs parents to let children follow their impulses in order to avoid stifling creativity. If this method is bad for a son, it is disastrous for a daughter, who, by nature, tends more toward following her emotions.

If you want your daughter to be pure and practice the Commandments, she must begin early to learn to govern her sensibilities, to check her imagination, and to judge her impulses to see if they are good or bad. The unchecked imagination is like an addictive drug, and it may very well end by leading your daughter away from the good, upright path.

A mother should also cultivate the proper idea of love in her daughters. Girls are moved by emotions more than boys are. Therefore, it is very important for them to begin to understand that love is not an absolute in itself. Today the Revolution stresses that love is everything. As long as you act out of love, anything is "fine." Such love is based on a false notion of charity, and it is wrong.

Catholics know that we must choose whom we love and that there is a hierarchy of love. In our Catechism, one of the first things we learn is that we must love God above all things, with our whole heart, soul, and mind. Therefore, we should not love anything that does not please God. We cannot love indiscriminately. Love must be subordinate to reason.

Let us consider an example. Meghan loves her brother Dominic, but she must realize that an authentic love has boundaries. She loves him with the aim of helping him to follow God's laws and get to Heaven. Therefore, she cannot encourage or be complicit with him in bad actions. To tell a lie to protect him from punishment may endear her to him, but it is not true love.

The feminine intuition of a girl is already in play at a very young age. A man by nature is more logical; a woman follows her intuitions. A woman's intuition is definitely something to take into consideration. It is often correct, but not always. A mother should begin to train her daughter to recognize that this intuition can be helpful, but that it is not infallible. It is a kind of lottery with a 50/50 chance of winning.

So, begin to teach your daughter to check that first impulse, and to be sure that the thing which enthuses her is good, correct, and in line with the principles of Catholic Morals.

Otherwise, your daughter can end up living by impulses in everything, never checking to see if the impulse coincides with reality. This "reality check" is very important today since the Revolution tries to encourage a girl to follow her impulses, with the aim of inducing her to adopt its bad fashions. Unless she has good criteria to apply for judging things correctly, she can fall into the trap of following revolutionary customs and trends.

Obviously, one of the worst enemies of developing good criteria for girls is the television. Remember, your daughter is much more influenced than your son by impressions of persons and their ways of being and dressing. Your son watches a cowboy movie and sees the action. Your daughter sees everything else, especially anything having to do with a girl in the story. She knows the color of her hair; she can describe the dress, bonnet, and shoes she was wearing; she can imitate the inflection of her voice or accent.

What does your daughter see on television today? She sees girls in immoral clothing, the use of sassy or impertinent language, vulgarities and crass modern customs, immoral romances, intrigues and subterfuges, etc. These ways of being will influence the way she sees and reacts to the world more than you realize.

They can also distort her notion of reality. She watches a program and admires the leading star – "He is such a good man." She is not mature enough to discern that the man is an actor playing a role, that, in fact, he is a bad person who follows an immoral lifestyle. No, he is wonderful. This inability to distinguish appearance from reality leads young girls to foolishly and mindlessly follow the movie idol or rock star of the moment.

Neither overindulgence nor excessive severity

A wise mother avoids two extremes with her daughter. The first is overindulgence. Do not indulge her every fancy. If you do everything she wants and give in to all her little whims, by the time she is in her teens she will be wearing the popular indecent fashions, going to places and parties that are not wholesome, and being part of the pleasure-oriented teen subculture of our day.

If you wait until then to correct her, it will be too late. She will be accustomed to having her own way and will rebel against your restraints and discipline. Your earlier indulgence for her seemingly innocent desires will have a damaging effect on her later life.

On the other hand, it is also possible for a mother to fall into the opposite extreme – an exaggerated severity, transforming the home into a sad, dark, joyless dwelling.

"Mother, may I have a new dress?" "No, it is not necessary, you already have three."

Annette expresses a desire for a small bottle of perfume. "Absolutely not! You're becoming worldly!"

Is she spending too much time combing her hair in front of the mirror? The mother spanks her to punish her vanity.

This puritanical spirit, which has an excessive fear of the legitimate comforts and pleasures of life, can lead to disorders in daughters as readily as overindulgence does.

If you exercise this constant severity, your daughter will obey you at first out of fear. But do not be surprised when she begins to hide her desires from you because she is afraid you will forbid them. And often she will find a way to experiment with the forbidden fruit in secret. Such over-severity breaks the confidence she should have in you and can lead to revolt against you.

Recourse to Our Lady

A mother who denies her daughter pretty dresses with lace, hair ribbons, or simple accessories because she does not want her to become vain and worldly is not prudent. By these harsh restrictions she can create an inordinate desire for such things in her daughter, who feels deprived and confused. Is she bad to want a white patent purse like Alice's? In fact, she is not.

The wise mother, who wants her daughter to develop refined taste, as well as correct judgment, will rejoice to see her new dress and will not condemn her for her feminine desire to have pretty things. Instead, she will encourage and help her daughter to dress properly and elegantly: "That dress is such a lovely shade of blue. I'm sure it will be a good color for you. Why don't you try it on?"

A mother who wants love and respect from her daughter must practice goodness in her treatment of her. She avoids a sharp and imperious tone in her voice and manners. She understands that at times, if discipline and principle are not involved, it is better to shut her eyes to some caprices of her child. She prays often to Our Lady to know what to encourage or avoid, what to permit or forbid.

If she provides security for her children, it is because her anchor and guide is the Virgin Mary, the Mother *par excellence,* She goes to Our Lady often during the day, asking for her goodness and a supernatural love for her children.

If she feels insecure and uncertain, she asks for the grace of certainty and firmness in dealing with her children. If she is choleric and tends to admonish too much, she asks for the grace to be calm and measured in her punishments. If she is overprotective and too proud of her children, she asks for the grace to be vigilant and objective in order to help her children overcome their defects and conquer their vices, enabling them to fulfill their vocations and reach their final home in Heaven.

St. Gregory the Great spoke of the government of souls as the art of arts. A mother is specially called to share in that art by fashioning the souls of her children.

* * *

Chapter VI

At the Table

We are of the old school that believes nothing is more destructive to courtesy than the notion that two completely different standards of manners can exist: company manners and home manners. That is to say, if you are going out or having company, you sit straight, hold the fork properly, and converse congenially. But, if it is "only" family, you can slouch, forget the silverware, and basically do and say whatever you want.

It is this second school that fosters the notion that etiquette is all show and theater. How many times has our natural, spontaneous American scoffed at the rules of good breeding as hypocritical because he sees persons who are cavalier in public and barbarian at home. In his flawed reasoning he thinks, "Better to be honest and barbarian all the time." The Catholic spirit – tending to perfection and excellence in everything – comes to a different conclusion: It is better to be civilized at all times.

To achieve this admirable aim, courtesy must be learned and practiced regularly at home. One of the most important places to do so is at the table, where the family gathers daily for meals.

The earliest courtesy books dedicated many pages to *do's and don'ts* at the table. In George Washington's *Rules of Civility*, for example, more than half of the 110 rules apply to table behavior. Why? It is because the family meal is the earliest classroom in courtesy, the place of our first lessons in manners. For the civilized man, how he eats is as important as what he eats.

Table rules are not senseless and archaic. The good table manners of Christian Civilization came into being based on an authentic respect for God, others, and ourselves:

- *A respect for God*: Every meal – breakfast, lunch, or dinner – begins and ends with a prayer, an acknowledgement of

God, Who gave us the food we eat and Who holds the first place in our thoughts and lives.

• *A respect for others*: Courtesy calls us to show consideration for the rights and feelings of everyone at the table. We don't chew with our mouths open, make strange noises, criticize the food, or reach across the table to grab the bread because we don't want to annoy the ones we love. We want to act in a way that increases their pleasure to be with us.

• *A respect for ourselves*: Sitting down clean and neatly dressed to a properly set table, eating with civility, and conversing amiably remind us of our dignity.

Slowing down and eating together

If we are too busy to set the table, if breakfast is a rushed affair, if lunch is veritably nonexistent, and if everyone is going here and there at dinnertime, it is time to re-establish our priorities. Following the "eat on the go" habit, we are paying tribute to the Revolution – even unconsciously.

The bedlam of modern life has fostered a chaotic and revolutionary lifestyle where fewer families are eating together.

One of the goals of this little book is to invite Catholics to a counter-revolutionary attitude. They should free up time in their busy day to eat with their family. At the table they should counter chaos with order, the vulgar spirit with distinction, and spontaneous behavior with disciplined habits. Instead of allowing the Revolution to enter their homes and destroy their family lives, they should develop their own Catholic ambiences to influence a new society.

To achieve this goal, the starting point is to insist that the family eat together at the table. It is a requisite for any serious family life. The family must come together, not just to eat, but for conversation and to enjoy each other's company.

Let us remember that we are sociable creatures and that the enjoyment of eating and conversing together with our family is normally one of our first pleasures. Even King St. Louis IX of France put aside the weighty matters of State at his dinner table and insisted on lighter talk so that all could enjoy one another's company.

At what meal should we gather together? The ideal would be at every meal, but one may start with the main meal, either at midday or evening.

To help make your meal more civil and amiable, we will suggest some table manners that were developed in Christian Civilization. The reasons we will present for this or that rule are given to help you to understand and remember them. They demonstrate that table protocol is not composed of artificial conventions. Rather, the rules were introduced because they are sensible and wise.

A good ambience

The table and settings should be as attractive as possible. A pleasing appearance not only encourages good behavior, but also makes the meal more enjoyable.

The ideal is to have a clean tablecloth or placemats, a simple centerpiece or candles, matched china, a set of silverware, and gleaming glassware. The meal should be graciously served, be it a simple plate or an elaborate ensemble of courses.

How often this ideal is met depends on circumstances. Perhaps once a week, on Sunday, as well as on some special days of celebration, a formal table can be set. The effort will be well rewarded. Everyone's manners will improve, and adults and children will enjoy the formal setting and elegance.

Most Americans face the reality of a busy day with a shortage of time and no domestic help. In such circumstances, everyone can do what is possible to make a good ambience for meals. A clean tablecloth or place mats, a table neatly and properly set, folded napkins, a centerpiece, simple matched china or pottery, a set of stainless steel flatware – these things are achievable.

Many families have a special napkin ring for each child, so that cloth napkins can be used on a daily basis. Each one folds his napkin at the end of the meal and puts it back in his ring, and the napkins are washed once or twice a week. This is a very good custom. We know a gentleman who, when he was a boy, received a monogrammed napkin ring, which he continues to use on a daily basis.

One important way to maintain a fine eating ambience is to prevent the family table from becoming a catch-all. The table is not a coat rack or closet. A table stacked with books, newspapers, or art and science projects gives the impression that the meal is a secondary thing.

This spirit of disorder soon spreads. The silverware and plates are set haphazardly on the table. Several empty glasses sit in one corner. Mary spills her milk on a pile of Mother's recipes. Before it reaches this point, the father should make it clear he does not appreciate the conglomeration on the table: "Martha, please remove your homework." Or, "George, we don't appreciate having your soldiers making war on the table. Let's clear it so we can have dinner."

Many families who home-school find it convenient to use the family table for doing class work. In principle, it is better to have school studies and dining in two separate rooms. It is opportune for a child studying all morning in one room to change ambiences when he takes a break – a snack or refreshment in the kitchen or at the dinner table, for example. If children study at the table, it becomes very tempting to leave books or various projects on the tabletop and eat around them.

Sometimes, however, the family home does not provide a variety of options. There might be only one large table available for both study and meals. In this case, organize your school schedule so that one hour before the meal, the children stop studying and put away their books and homework in a separate place. The table must be cleared of books, cleaned, and set for the meal.

To create a family ambience, the first commandment is to turn off the television. Another modern inconvenience at meals is the cell phone. It should be turned off during the dinner hour, and the answering machine should take incoming calls.

If the father, the mother, or an adult in the house is expecting an important call, of course it can be taken. In this case, he or she should apologize, rise from the table, and receive the phone call in another room in order to avoid disrupting those who are at table. But a child should never answer the phone or be excused from the table to do so. There is, after all, a hierarchy in the home.

The basic table setting

"Why do we have these rules?" is one question we are often asked. Most table-related customs came about to help meals run more smoothly, enhance the food and drink, and give more consideration to everyone at the table.

Another question frequently posed is, "How is the table properly set for everyday meals?" What we propose to do here is to present a typical table setting, with the understanding that there are variations and different styles – both here and in other countries.

Let us set a basic table. The napkins are clean, folded and flat, and laid to the left of the plate. For formal meals, they can be more elaborately folded and set on each plate.

The water glass is above the plate to the right, at the tip of the knife. If you are serving a wine, the wine glass is placed slightly below and to the right of the water glass. With regard to the placement of the glasses, what is the reason for this rule? The water goblet is normally the taller piece of glassware. To avoid the potential of spilling, the smaller glass is placed on the outside.

The formula for the daily table setting is simple and easy to memorize: knives to the right of the plate, forks to the left. The reason for this rule is that the silverware setting was conceived for right-handed people. Thus, the knife, which needs to be used with more strength when we cut a piece of meat, goes to the right; consequently, the fork goes to the left.

The sharp edge of the knife faces the plate to keep you from cutting yourself when picking up the other utensils. The forks are set with the prongs up. If you are dining in some places in Europe, however, it is considered proper to set the forks with the tines down.

A person normally eats the soup with his right hand, so the soup spoon is set to the right of the knife.

If soup is being served, the soup bowl is placed in the center of the plate. Never set a soup bowl on the bare tablecloth or placemat. Rather, place the soup bowl over the meal plate, even if the latter will not be used. It gives you a place to rest the spoon after using it.

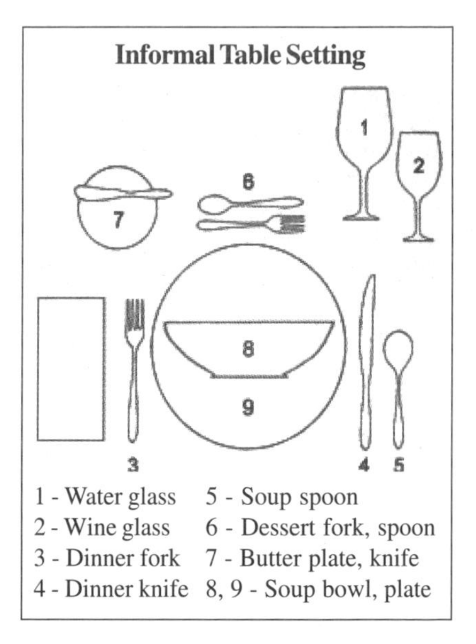

Informal Table Setting

1 - Water glass
2 - Wine glass
3 - Dinner fork
4 - Dinner knife
5 - Soup spoon
6 - Dessert fork, spoon
7 - Butter plate, knife
8, 9 - Soup bowl, plate

To set a soup bowl straight on the table is as unacceptable as placing a coffee cup without the saucer on the tablecloth. The coffee spoon needs a saucer to rest on; otherwise your clean tablecloth will soon have stains.

The dessert fork and spoon are placed above the plate following the same rule as the meal silverware. Here is a simple way to remember which way the dessert silverware is placed: the spoon moves up from the spoon side, the fork moves up from the fork side. The fork is closest to the plate. The dessert silverware can also be brought to the table with the dessert.

If coffee or tea is served after dessert, the spoons are placed on the saucers.

The basic rule for silverware is to set only the utensils that will be used during the meal. Let the meal dictate what pieces of the silverware you lay out. If you are having soup and crackers, all you need is a spoon and butter knife at each plate. A fork can suffice for a simple salad meal.

The formal table setting: the glassware

It is good for the adults and older children in the family to be familiar with setting a formal table. If you know the proper setting for an elaborate, multi-course meal, you will be prepared for every social occasion.

For a formal dinner, the water glass is set above the knife, and the wine glasses are placed to its right in the order of their use. You may note that the glasses line up in descending order of size, which is convenient for avoiding spills.

They can be set either in a row parallel to the edge of the table or at a diagonal, depending on the number of glasses and the other utensils you have on the table.

Some improvisation is permitted, should your line become too long. The champagne flute can be placed above the three wine glasses.

This would be the line up at a typical banquet:

- The white wine glass, which is smaller, is on the outside and is used with the fish course;
- The red wine glass, which is larger, is used with the meat course;
- The champagne glass, the tallest, is used with the dessert.
- The water glass, to the left of the wine glasses, is above the knife.

Wine, like every drink, is poured from the right. Do not pour across the table. Perhaps at formal dinners, your eldest son could serve the dinner wine at the table. Every gentleman should know how to pour wine.

Always remember that crystal should be spotless. Each glass should be washed and dried with a lint-free cotton or linen cloth before being laid on the table by its stem. This is a fitting job for older children, who will not only learn to handle the fine stemware, but also have the satisfaction of seeing shining crystal on a well-set table.

The formal table setting: the silverware

Silverware for a meal with courses is set so that the person can confidently work from the outside in, following the order of the courses, with the knives set to the right of the plate and the forks to the left.

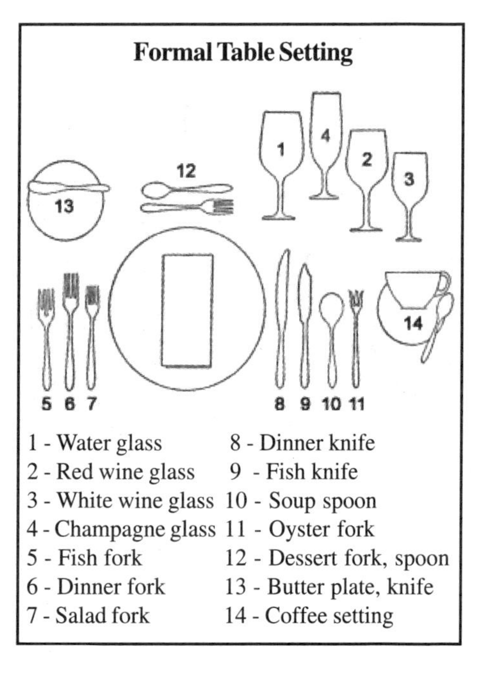

Formal Table Setting

Silverware on the left of the plate (working from outside in) includes a fish fork, a meat course fork, and a salad fork (placed this way when salad is served after the main course).

On the right of the plate are a soup spoon, a fish knife, and a dinner knife. If a seafood appetizer is served, an oyster fork is placed to the right of the soup spoon – it is the only fork set on the 'spoon side.'

If the salad is served before the fish course, the salad fork is placed to the left of the fish fork. The butter knife is set on the bread plate. The dessert fork and spoon are positioned above the plate, as described earlier.

We assume most families will not be using multiple forks and knives at family meals, but, as noted above, it is good to be familiar with the placements. On special occasions it is worthwhile to make an effort to set a full table so that no one in your family will bc intimidated by a line-up of glasses and silverware when he or she is invited to a formal dinner.

A few extras

A service plate, also called a charger or *serviette*, is a larger plate used under the dishes for the appetizer, salad, or soup courses. It is removed when the entrée on the dinner plate is brought to the table. Its purpose is not just decorative. Its aim is to protect the table so it is fresh and clean when the main course is served.

If you are serving a wine with the meal, a salad dressed with vinegar should be served after the main course because it introduces a strong acid taste in the palate that remains for a long time. The taste of any fine wine that you serve will be adulterated by that vinegar. For this reason, people from countries who appreciate wine during meals eat their salads at the end, before the fruit and the dessert.

People who do not generally drink wine with their meals usually take the salad at the beginning because the vinegar in the salad dressing has the effect of stimulating the appetite. Recently, many Americans have begun to develop their taste for wine with meals. Therefore, we recommend that they adopt the traditions that enhance the appreciation of the wine and food by beginning to serve the salad after the main course when there is wine at the table.

When the salad is served before the main course, its plate – a smaller one especially designed for that purpose – is set on top of the main plate or the charger. If it is served after the main course, the salad plate is brought to the table and replaces the larger plate when the latter is removed from the table.

A bread and butter plate, if used, is placed above and slightly to the left of the forks. The well-mannered person breaks off a piece of bread to eat and butters it from the pat he has placed on the bread plate.

This rule of breaking bread into morsels goes back to Old Testament times, when it was the custom for table leavings to be collected after the meal and given to the poor. In consideration for those who would receive the leftovers, one broke off only what he would eat from the bread. The memory of such commendable charity still justifies the existence of this rule today.

Serving the meal

There are many ways to serve the meal, all acceptable and open to variations that best suit a home and family. These are the basic methods:

Restaurant style: The plates are filled in the kitchen before they are placed on the table. Serve from the left side, and remove the used dishes from the right.

American style: The food is served on platters and in serving dishes that are passed after everyone is seated and grace is said. Food is passed counter-clockwise at the table, from left to right. If you know the practical reason for this, you will not forget the rule. It is to allow the next person to take the dish with his left hand and serve himself from it with his right.

French style: Servers present platters of food to seated guests who serve themselves. Few families today have a kitchen staff to serve meals French style. So that your family knows how it should be done, it is a good idea to let the older children practice serving a Sunday or special meal.

Here are a few fundamental rules: Serve from the left side. The person being served takes the serving fork in the left hand and the spoon in the right. After serving himself, he puts the spoon and fork back side-by-side on the platter. Normally every person takes at least a small portion from the plate being offered, but it is permitted to refuse a plate with a polite excuse: "Thank you. It looks very good, but I believe I will pass."

English style: After prayers before the meal, the host or hostess carves the meat at the table and serves each plate, adds the vegetables, then passes the plates down the table. When all are served, the guests begin to eat. If you pass your plate back to the head of the table for a second helping, remove the knife and fork. If a resting utensil is not offered, lay down your fork, prongs up, and place the blade of your knife between two of the prongs, so that only a small part of the silverware touches the tablecloth.

Buffet style: The food is placed on a buffet table or sideboard. Family members and guests serve themselves. Grace is said either before or after all are served. Before beginning to eat, wait until all are seated with their plates in front of them, unless the hostess indicates otherwise.

Seating at the table

In a home, everyone generally has his own place at the table. In a home with a sense of hierarchy, that place has a meaning. The father sits at the head. His wife sits at his right or at the other end of the table, if this is more convenient for a practical reason. The eldest child sits at the left of the head of the table, and so on.

If there is a guest, there should not be a haphazard reshuffling of seats or cries of "Let me sit by Aunt Jane!" "No, it's my turn!" The father or the mother will assign the guest a seat, and the children will take their places, following the father's directive. Children should realize that there is a proper place for everyone, a place decided by their parents – not one that follows their whims and fancies.

The traditional place of honor is to the right of the host; the next one is to the right of the hostess when she is seated at the other end of the table. But certainly, there can be adaptations, depending on the guest and the family customs.

The head of the family should not relinquish his place at the table, even to a very distinguished guest or a member of the clergy. A Bishop or priest should be seated either at the other end of the table or at the place of honor – to the right of the host.

In order to improve the level of the conversation, a good rule is to alternate men and women at the table. This rule applies more to social events, but it may also be used at family dinners.

Beginning the meal

When called to the table, everyone should come promptly. This shows basic courtesy to the lady of the house, who has prepared the meal and taken care that it should be served hot and at its best. If Mark dawdles fifteen minutes or a half-hour to finish his homework, the meal can be ruined. Some families ring a dinner bell – a first warning bell to notify family members to clean up and prepare for the meal, and a second bell five minutes later that marks the beginning of the meal.

If the mother asks James to call everyone to supper, he should not stand in the main hallway and yell at the top of his voice, "Time to eat!" This is not civil behavior. He should pass by the occupied rooms announcing, "Dinner is served. Please come to the table."

Everyone should arrive at the table with hands washed and hair combed. Parents must set an example if they want their children to adopt higher standards. If a father comes to dinner in a T-shirt or in jogging clothes, what can be expected of the sons? If, on the other hand, a father puts on a jacket for dinner, the sons will learn to acquire this fine habit.

With all standing quietly behind their chairs, the grace is said by the head of the family. If the father is not present, the mother leads the prayer. Children should learn the beginning and ending meal prayers by hearing them said by their parents. It is more in accordance with the spirit of hierarchy for only one person to say grace, while the others follow in silence, rather than to have a "communitarian participation." The egalitarian custom of having children create improvised verses of thanksgiving should be avoided, as should the habit of joining and holding hands.

After prayers, everyone is seated. A man customarily helps the lady on his left to be seated. But it is a very fine custom for the eldest son to pull out his mother's chair for her. Brothers should be taught to seat their sisters, who should receive this kindness gracefully. If a girl does not have a boy on her right, she should seat herself. The seating process should not be an acrobatics show with the boys racing around the table to seat all the girls in an exaggerated display of politesse. It should be done naturally.

To seat a lady is a very simple matter. The man moves the chair just far enough back for the lady to stand in front of it. Then as she begins to seat herself, he pushes it gently under her. It need not be done with a grand manner or flourish. Seating the ladies should become a simple, natural courtesy. A man will never have to experience an awkward or embarrassing moment at a formal dinner if he knows what is expected of him.

Once seated, take your napkin, unfold it, and place it on your lap. The European custom for men to tuck the napkin under the left side of the collar is perfectly proper. It serves the function of protecting the tie from becoming stained should food accidentally drop or spill during the meal.

Do not start eating until all have been served and the hostess begins. Even an important or prestigious guest waits for the hostess before he begins to eat. An admirable practice in many homes is that no one begins to eat until the lady of the house has lifted her fork. We highly recommend this simple courtesy paid to the one who has gone to so much trouble to provide a fine meal.

At the table there is a proper way to use the napkin. Before taking a drink, pat the mouth lightly to remove grease or crumbs. Greasy glass marks are not appetizing. A lady should delicately dab the corners of her mouth to prevent lipstick from transferring to the napkin.

One never uses the napkin to clean the teeth, blow the nose, or catch sneezes. That is why you have a handkerchief – at least, we hope you have one. A boy should be accustomed to have a clean white handkerchief in his pocket, and a young lady should also have one ready at hand. We knew a European lady who used to say she could always spot an American man at the table – he was the one without a handkerchief. Always carrying a handkerchief is one custom we hope will again become the norm.

Some basics of table manners

There are certain rudimentary laws at the table that all adults and children over age eight are expected to follow:

• Sit erect at the table. The unused hands may be placed in your lap, according to the English style. The French style teaches us to keep both unused hands at the edge of the table on either side of the plate. Both are perfectly acceptable. In any case, never eat or rest with your elbows on the table.

• Do not slump in the chair; even worse is to lean back and rock in it. It is not permitted to bend the head and body down to the food – a sign of sloth and primitive manners. Rather, the food is brought up to the mouth.

• Never reach across the table for a dish; ask the person nearest you to pass it. Always say *please* when asking for something, and then do not forget to say *thank you*. You always pass the salt and pepper shakers together in order to keep the pieces side-by-side for the next person who requests them.

• If the pitcher or dish you are passing has a handle, turn the handle toward the person receiving it. A small gesture like this is a way to show consideration to others at the table.

• Eat slowly, chewing the food well with the mouth closed. Wipe the lips and have no food in the mouth before drinking.

• Do not talk with your mouth full. One advantage of taking small bites is that if you are asked a question, you can finish chewing, swallow, and answer without gulping or taking a long time before responding.

• Do not make any unseemly noises with the mouth – slurping coffee, smacking lips, snorting, and so on. Water should be taken without sounds. If a person has the bad habit of making some sound, he should correct this defect by training himself to take small sips instead of large mouthfuls. Some modern fathers have the mistaken idea that making vulgar sounds is amusing or in some way manly. They are mistaken. Such behavior is always rude and insulting to the others at the table. The real man is a gentleman at all times.

• Cover your mouth with your hand when yawning, coughing, or sneezing. If you have a handkerchief, blowing the nose is permitted at the table, but it should be carried out quickly and unobtrusively.

• Keep the fingers away from inside the mouth, ears, and nose. Do not dislodge food from your teeth with your fingers or a toothpick. If some food particle is trapped and bothers you, excuse yourself and go to the bathroom to use a toothpick or dental floss.

• If you have to leave the table during the meal, always excuse yourself. This formula works perfectly for children, "May I please be excused?" A child should wait for permission from one of the adults before leaving.

• Never put your own silverware into a serving dish, e.g., your knife in the butter, your spoon in the jam, your fork on the meat platter, and so on.

• If you place something inedible in your mouth, do not spit it out or force yourself to swallow it. Place it back on your fork, and discreetly put it on the rim of your plate. This is perfectly correct behavior. Whatever you put in your mouth with your fingers – olive seeds, fruit pits, etc. – you can remove with your fingers (unobtrusively, of course).

• It is a lack of consideration for others when ladies apply or correct their makeup at the table. Use your compact or lipstick in the bathroom. Some girls have the disagreeable habit of playing with their hair, twisting a strand around their fingers or flipping it behind an ear. Touching hair and food never mix, and it is repulsive to the well-bred person to be obliged to watch this behavior.

• Everyone should remain at the table until the meal is finished. If someone wants to leave the table before the others, he should ask to be excused.

The courses – starting with appetizer and soup

If an appetizer is served, it is brought to the table first. Use the oyster fork (also called the cocktail fork) for this hors-d'oeuvre, often a shrimp cocktail or oyster plate. When you have finished the course, lay the fork on the plate under the appetizer dish.

Soup is served next. A quite accomplished businessman once passed up the soup course because he did not know how to eat it properly. There is no reason that anyone in your family should ever miss a good soup. All you need to know are a few basics:

• The soup spoon is held between your thumb and index finger. It is very disagreeable to see children – yes, and even adults! – holding the spoon like a toothbrush.

• Take your spoon, start at the rim of bowl closest to you, then spoon *away from you* toward the middle of the bowl until your spoon is filled. Then, lift the spoon slightly over the plate – so that any drops can fall back into the soup – and bring it to your mouth. The mouth should be open enough to receive the spoon, but not wide open as if you were in the dentist's chair.

• Do not overfill the spoon and never blow on it. If it is too hot to eat, wait until the soup cools in the spoon. If you have a firm hand, it is permitted to carefully move the spoon up and down to cool its content. Lift the spoon to your mouth (do not put your face in the bowl), and sip the soup from the side of the spoon. Your hand rises slightly above your lips, allowing the soup to flow easily into your mouth. In making this movement, avoid lifting your elbow so that you do not accidentally hit your neighbor to the right. This procedure, carried out correctly, prevents the need to slurp your soup – an always reproachable act.

- If the soup is good and you want to enjoy the last sip, tilt the bowl away from you. The reason for this is to prevent drips from splashing onto your clothing. When you notice a person tilting the bowl toward him, it is a sure sign that he was never taught proper table manners.

- Between sips, you can leave the spoon in the soup bowl – this is called resting. If the soup is served in a cup, you should rest the spoon on the saucer. When you have finished, the spoon can be left in the soup bowl, but never in a soup cup. Iin the latter case, leave it on the side of the soup plate.

The salad course

We have already discussed some points on salad. There are still several others to consider.

Since in America salad is usually served before the main course, we decided to deal with it now, after the soup course.

Do not use the dinner knife to cut your salad; save it for the main course. You should be able to cut the salad with the salad fork, one bite at a time.

When you have finished, lay the fork on the plate with the tines pointing upward to the 10 o'clock position. This is the standard finish position, indicating that the plate can be taken away. Do not be surprised, however, if a European guest lays the fork facing down on the plate – this is the continental style. Both are acceptable.

By the way, if you make a mistake in using the silverware – you use the main fork instead of the salad fork – just keep eating. Do not apologize for your error or change in mid-course. Never point out your own or someone else's mistake, even if you have a good intention: "Mother, Jeremy used the wrong fork for his salad. Should I bring him another one?"

The main course is served

In the United Sates, it is quite unusual to serve a fish course before a meat course – one or the other is served as the main course. When the main course is served, use the larger knife and fork. The knife is for cutting or to help bring some food to the fork. Indeed, sometimes there are some stubborn peas that do not want to embark onto your fork for their last journey, and the knife can help bring them there.

A gentleman does not hold a fork filled with food up in mid-air to make a point in the conversation or wave it around exuberantly. Once the fork has taken hold of the food, keep it down if you are talking until you decide to bring it to your mouth.

What is worse is to hold the fork like a shovel. Unfortunately today we see many young persons in restaurants who still do not know how to hold a fork properly. Really, it is an embarrassment for the family because it reveals poor formation. Hold the fork by resting it on the middle finger and using the thumb and index finger to balance it. With the prongs turned up, bring it to the mouth.

In the American style of eating, after cutting one piece of meat, the knife is placed at the top of the plate, blade facing toward the center of the plate. The fork is transferred to the right hand, tines up, and the bite is eaten. One piece at a time is the rule. If the meat does not require cutting, eat it with the fork in the right hand.

Some things are considered appropriate to eat with your fingers: appetizers on crackers or toast, celery or carrot sticks, bite-sized cakes or cookies, and, of course, bread.

Americans have the custom of eating fried chicken, spare ribs, French fries, and onion rings with their fingers. We propose that they stop doing so. Europeans always eat these items at the table with forks and knives. We suggest using this more refined method.

If you are serving a lobster or hard-shelled crab or oysters with the various utensils for extracting the meat, you will obviously have to use your fingers to hold the shell, pull on the claws, and help draw out the meat. Yes, even a well-mannered Frenchman does the same.

Afterward, finger bowls with hot water are offered to clean the fingertips and lips. Or a tray with hot, wet napkins or hand sanitizing towelettes are presented to attain the same result. At times you may find a slice of lemon or lime in the finger bowl, since its juice helps to remove the grease of your fingers. If a quarter of a lime arrives atop each hot, damp towel, this is to allow you to squeeze its juice over the towel and then wipe your fingers and lips.

Vegetables are eaten with the fork. If you need a little help getting them onto the fork, it is fine to use a piece of bread or your knife with your left hand. But whatever you do, do not use your fingers to shove the food onto the fork.

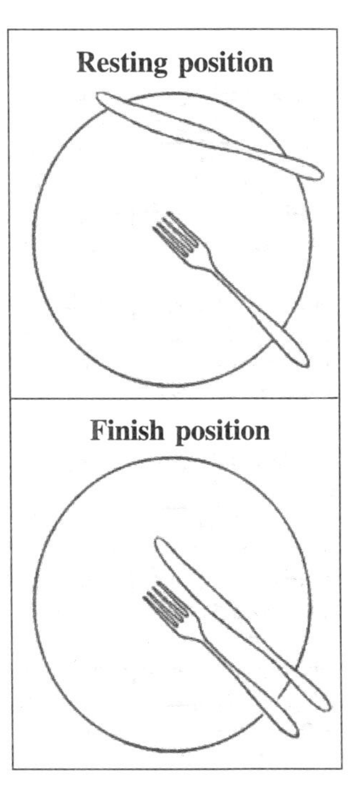

Should you be interrupted in the meal before you have finished eating, leave your silverware in the resting position: the knife on the upper rim of the plate, the fork on the right side. The well-mannered person who sees them in this position understands that you did not finish the course.

When you have finished the course, place the fork and knife in the finish position – that is, lay both the fork and knife parallel to each other on the plate with the tips pointing to the left. The fork is on the inside with prongs pointing up and the knife blade is facing the fork. This signals that you have completed the course

It is a general rule that you should never set a used piece of silverware back on the tablecloth or placemat. The obvious reason is that you do not want to soil the fabric, causing more work for the hostess.

Dessert and coffee

All the plates, serving dishes, and condiments should be cleared from the table before the dessert is served.

A dessert fork is used for pie or cake, a spoon for ice-cream, pudding, or crème brulée.

It is common to have a cheese plate or fruit for dessert or before the dessert. This is a very healthful and pleasant addition to a meal.

There is a certain order to follow for dessert plates. *First* come the cheeses because they are served with the same red wine you just used in the meat course. *Second* come the fruits, served before the sweet dessert to prevent them from tasting sour. *Third* comes the sweet dessert – the cake, pastry, ice-cream, or other traditional dessert.

Remember, if the cheese is round or triangular, cut off a slice as in a pie. If the cheese is in the shape of a square or rectangle and is a small cheese, cut the slices parallel to the edges; if it is a large cheese you follow the same pie-style cutting.

If fruits are served without silverware, such as grapes, plums, or apricots, you are supposed to eat them with your fingers. When you have finished, wipe your fingers with your napkin.

In the United States, coffee is often served at the end of the meal. The sugar and cream should be kept together and passed from left to right. One does not slurp the coffee or blow on it if it is too hot. After stirring it, the spoon is placed on the saucer. It is never left in the cup when you have finished.

After the dessert and coffee is the proper time for the guests or members of the family to thank the lady of the house, if they did not do so before: “Thank you for your nice dinner, Mrs. Brown.” Or, “Thank you for the good meal, Grandmother.”

Then the hostess signals the end of the meal by folding her napkin and placing it on the left side of the plate. Other formulas are also common. The hostess may say, “Shall we have coffee on the veranda?” or “Let’s continue the conversation in the living room,” or simply, “Thank you for your enjoyable company.”

All stand for the grace after meals. Each one tucks his chair back under the table so that the room is presentable and ready for the next meal.

Clearing the table

We know it is very handy for a busy, tired mother to scrape the plates and stack them right at the table, but it is not correct. If you want to accustom your children to courteous ways, it is necessary to make the extra effort and clear the table properly.

Plates should be cleared no more than two at a time – so that one piece is not piled on top of another – and then scraped and stacked out of view of the guests. As children get older, they should be assigned to clear the table. Doing things correctly gives children a sense of satisfaction and provides a good way to fight against laziness.

An extra advantage of good table manners

Good table manners practiced consistently yield the valuable advantage of self-confidence. A person who knows table conventions and is guided by the canons of etiquette will never feel insecure at any gathering.

Those with an egalitarian mindset do not like to admit it, but nothing reveals the background and breeding of a person more than his table manners. Acquiring them is a simple matter of practicing the table rules set out in this manual in your family home.

* * *

Chapter VII

The Art of Conversation in the Home

Three times a day the family gathers around the table to eat. In the Catholic home it is a place not just to feed the body, but to also nourish the soul – culturally, intellectually, and spiritually. It is a place of formation, where the art of conversation is normally learned. It is a haven where a person finds enjoyment and entertainment.

In a family that converses amiably and intelligently at home, the children naturally learn the art of conversation. Those who do not receive a good formation in their homes, however, often find it necessary to enroll in conversation courses – a product of the modern age.

It was probably the case that their family members sat in front of the television during meals or ate on the run. The conversation – when there was any – was doubtlessly banal or vulgar. So, when traveling or faced with new social circumstances, these ill-formed youths are awkward and sadly at a loss for words.

Setting the tone

Conversation is meant to please and entertain; at the same time, it should instruct and feed the spirit with bits and pieces that improve the intellectual, cultural, and spiritual life. To achieve this end, there was a rule once so ingrained in civilized family life that it did not need to be written down. It was understood that the adults should set the tone for the conversation in the home and at the table.

The plummeting level of table talk in so many homes today is a direct result of a child-centered mentality, which causes insecure parents to assume that everything, inluding the conversation, must revolve around the children. At the dinner table, parents are obliged to show an interest in every precious word that little

Michael says so that he will feel loved and appreciated as an equally valued member of the household. This is not the correct way to maintain hierarchy in the Catholic home.

But how do you have a good conversation? We will provide a brief explanation and an example.

A good conversation is primarily a disinterested exchange of facts, observations, and opinions about things we know and want to communicate to our neighbor.

Mr. Howard likes to read about the history and customs of European nations in order to understand the psychology of the different peoples. For quite some time he has developed this interest and has made many observations about the French, Germans, Spanish, and Anglo-Saxons.

It is normal for him to communicate his findings to his wife and older children. The table is the right place to do so.

"Do you know, I was thinking about what would be the main characteristic of the French psychology," he begins the conversation one evening. "I believe it is the courtesy they were known for in the past. I think this is the reason why France came to be the most influential country in Europe.

"After the French Revolution, however, France lost the faith. The people became insecure and, consequently, aggressive and arrogant. One result is that France lost much of her former influence and prestige. Today, when we visit there we are treated very rudely by almost everyone."

He goes on to relate an incident that occurred in the market when his parents were in Paris several years ago. This topic raises questions and comments from the others at the table.

"What an interesting point, Mark," Mrs. Howard remarks. Then she recalls a dessert her aunt used to make called the *île flottante*. "That means floating island," she explains. "It is a round island of meringue that floats on a sea of custard. It is a marvelous dessert, reflecting this good side of the French. I believe I will look for that recipe and make it so that we can experience refinement in practice."

After dinner, Thomas, one of the younger children, who did not fully understand the conversation at the table, asks Ann, his older sister, "Where is France? Can you tell me something about it?"

Ann, who remembers the beautiful picture of Sainte-Chapelle in a book in the library, goes to get it and shows it to her little brother. "This chapel was built by St. Louis IX to house the Crown of Thorns. Look at the marvelous colors," she tells him.

Bernard enters the conversation with another piece of information, "You may not know this, but my name saint, St. Bernard, was from France, and Father says he was the model of French courtesy. He wrote the *Salve Regina*, one of the most beautiful prayers we have."

In this way, by sharing his observations on one of his favorite subjects, the father engaged the whole family in an exercise to increase their knowledge of French culture. From that moment on, French courtesy and rudeness entered the repertoire of interesting topics to be discussed at the table.

Another day Mr. Howard makes an observation about the Cossacks of the Crimea, affirming that they were the greatest masters of horsemanship in the world. He shows the table some pictures he has to support his point. Yet another day he discusses the Spanish spirit of combative militancy that is expressed by the *torero*, the bullfighter.

One can understand that when a family discusses many such topics at its daily dinners, the family table becomes a center of culture, history, art, and religion. No one wants to miss a meal where these interesting topics will be addressed.

These are examples of adult-centered conversation.

Now, as a study in contrast, imagine a child-centered conversation. Mr. Wall asks each child how his or her day was.

"Today I colored bunnies in class," says 5-year-old Bobby. "Oh, bunnies... How nice, Bobby. What color did you make them?"

"I made them blue." "Ah, very good ..."

This kind of talk attracts no one. It is the death of an interesting conversation. It is tedious for the adults and stimulates pride in the children. We agree that children are important, but we believe that for their good formation it is crucial to avoid child-centered conversations at the table. Children have to learn that they must adapt to the level of adults. Unfortunately, today, what we see more often is adults adapting themselves to the level of children.

You have, therefore, an elementary rule for conversation at the table: The tone must be set by the adults, primarily the father. Do not establish the revolutionary custom of child-centered conversation. Such talks should be reserved for other times, when the mother is alone with her child.

Another rule is a consequence of the first: Children should not speak at will at the dinner table but should follow the conversation of the adults, entering the talk when they are invited and when they have something of interest to say. They should strive to make their responses and comments at an adult level.

It is common today to find manuals that encourage parents to do the exact opposite: They should never appear bored, angry, or shocked at anything their children say at the table. Do not follow these manuals. Instead of forming children to be mature adults, they turn adults into children.

Topics of conversation

The table is not a time for endless comic stories and foolishness. Nothing is worse than a dinner table where the father acts as a kind of comedian, telling jokes and making puns to amuse everyone. It will not be long before his children and wife will tire of this behavior and cease to take him seriously. He will soon be the only one laughing at his jokes.

Appropriate topics of conversation are numberless. A conversation can travel from the weather to Mozart, then on to gardening or national politics. There is no need to stay on one topic. Music, art, good manners, theater, politics, languages, food, ambiences, décor – the topics are unlimited.

"I remember the plate of mussels I had in Belgium," says Mr. Hodges. And then follows a description of the ingredients, the way it was presented, the attentive waiter who served it, the observation of how the Belgians spoke in low voices in the crowded restaurant so that the music could be heard, and so on.

"Today we saw some of the most unusual colors of roses at the Tea Garden," Mrs. Miller says. "I especially liked the Betty Harkness rose because of its deep tangerine color and its strong, lovely perfume. Which one was your favorite, Margaret?"

Most conversations at the table consist of miscellaneous topics, entirely spontaneous, starting with the small common things of everyday life and passing through comments on the news of the day or onto even more lofty themes of a doctrinal character. What is important is that they take place in a natural and tranquil atmosphere.

Lessons in life

If other family members or friends are present at a gathering, the topics can normally generate discussions on politics, art, or religion. There is nothing wrong with a discussion in which different opinions are presented on controversial topics. However, even when voices rise as points are made, cordiality should be the rule.

Personal attacks must always be avoided, and the debate should remain in the realm of principles. If one party becomes too passionate or stubborn, preventing the conversation from reaching a cordial conclusion, one of the parties or the host should end the discussion, suggesting that it be postponed until later to avoid annoying the others present at the table.

When courtesy reigns in the discussions of adults, the children instinctively learn how to act in their own conversations. If the talk is serious, the vocabulary elevated, the words well-measured, clearly articulated, and securely spoken, children will understand what is expected of them, and will strive to rise to that level.

Sitting at the table and following the various topics, they learn to judge the degree of importance of the various themes. A child will also learn to perceive how different family members think and to judge which positions have more value: "Uncle George speaks very well, but he always gives the same argument." "Aunt Barbara's stories usually have some good lesson." "I always want to hear what Grandfather will say."

From the beginning to the end of the meal, the conversation should yield lessons in life for both those who participate and those who listen.

When and how to make corrections

The family gathering or dinner meal where several adults are present is not the place for giving sermons or correcting the children – except, of course, for inexcusable blunders like putting the finger in the butter. A look from a vigilant mother is usually sufficient to silence a too loquacious child or cut short an indiscreet remark.

How does a mother achieve the respect and authority to make corrections with simply a stern look? Many young women today have this question. "I tell my boys to stop being silly, and they just roll their eyes," poor Mrs. Harding complains.

Here, we face the challenge that many hate to address: a change in our way of being. Courtesy calls us to set aside our casual and egalitarian manners and to adopt a more formal and ceremonial way of speaking and acting. When parents act maturely, speak in an elevated way, and dress with dignity, they naturally inspire respect from their children. Instead of presenting themselves as equals to their offspring, they assume their natural authority and exercise it as a responsibility before God.

Therefore, when the mother is the only adult at the table with her children, she takes advantage of that time to teach manners gently and benevolently: "Yes, I know you don't like squash, Philip. But it is bad manners to refuse the food that is served." "We don't reach across the table for the bread, Ann. Ask Daniel to pass it to you." "After you stir the sugar into your tea, Margaret, place the teaspoon on the saucer. This is the correct way."

Mindful of her children's natural tendencies, she helps them to overcome their defects and encourages their good points. Gerald is loquacious and likes to monopolize the conversation. He has just seen the movie *A Man for All Seasons* and is enthusiastically giving a detailed account of it.

"You're doing a fine job," she remarks when he takes a pause, "but let's give Joseph a chance to tell us what happened next." The words are accompanied by a look that lets him know he should be quiet and let others speak.

The child who interrupts, she corrects. The one who gives monosyllabic answers, she tries to draw out. The one who asks too many questions, she stops, reminding him that one person should not dominate the conversation. Guiding and directing the table conversation, she teaches her children to respect one another and treat each other with consideration and courtesy.

Young children eating apart

We know that this suggestion may not be feasible for many families, but we present it as am ideal model that can be reached for some today, and perhaps for others tomorrow.

In a home with infants and very young children, there should be two different times for meals: one for the small children who cannot understand conversation or follow the rules of courtesy, and another for the adults and the older children.

When the very little ones are at the table, the seriousness of the gathering and the benefits it can bring will normally diminish or vanish. Therefore, the youngest children should have their meals at an earlier time, supervised by the mother, a nanny, an older daughter, or other relative. When the fussing little ones are already fed and in another room playing or in bed, this is the meal time for the adults and older children.

There is another advantage to this system. The younger children will look forward to the day when they can be part of the adult table, and they will strive to follow the rules and standards that permit them to be there.

Some *Do's and Don'ts* in conversation

We will close this chapter on conversation at the table with some general rules to follow:

- Do not gossip or practice personal detraction, talking about other people in a demeaning or uncharitable way.
- Do not deal with business matters or financial questions during a family gathering or dinner. Such matters should be dealt with privately between the interested parties at other times, not at family meals.
- Parents should never argue in the presence of their children, especially in matters involving the children.
- Do not mock or belittle others at the table. Sarcasm is even worse, because it implies contempt and causes resentments.
- Do not correct or flatly contradict another in the middle of a conversation. If he makes a flagrant mistake in a moral or doctrinal matter, let him finish his argument, and then present the correct point amiably: "If you permit me to disagree, I believe that the Catholic Church teaches something different on this topic, which is ..."

• Do not touch upon prosaic matters: recounting the gory details about field dressing a deer or the stomach flu of Aunt Mildred spoils appetites.

• Do not bring up topics that could harm the innocence of children.

• Do not use the expressions, "Whew, I'm stuffed," or "I'm full." Do say: "I'm satisfied," or "That was an excellent meal."

• Do show appreciation for a good meal or for a feature in the table décor or setting. A sincere compliment is always appreciated: "The roast was delicious!" or "The magnolia blossoms look so pretty in that crystal bowl."

• Do not read at the table, unless you are alone. If the conversation is lacking, an amiable silence is preferable to reading in the presence of another.

• Do not use the television, cell phone or computer during a meal. Such electronic devices are incompatible with conversation, good manners, and family life.

These are a few rules taken from the rich treasury of Catholic tradition.

Having a sense of what to say and when to say it is just as important as following a set of rules. The art of conversation will develop naturally as one learns to value others and appreciate what they have to say.

Above all, we must have a consideration for our neighbor, respect him, and do all that we can to help him advance on the road toward fulfilling the vocation he received from God.

* * *

Conclusion

Courteous or Barbarian

On the cover of this book is a charming picture of Queen Astrid of Belgium, who is being greeted by a gentleman at the 1935 Brussels World Exhibition. At her side in uniform is her husband, King Leopold.

Raised as a Lutheran in Sweden, her homeland, Princess Astrid converted to Catholicism in 1930, after she had studied the Catholic Faith and become fully convinced of its truth. Her father-in-law, King Albert, said repeatedly on the day of Astrid's entrance into the Catholic Church, "I am very happy. Now the family is united in the one Faith."

Astrid became the most popular Queen in Belgian history. She was known for her goodness and charity. A strong moral support to her husband, she surrounded him with tenderness and devotion in a difficult period of political and economic crisis in Belgium and Europe. She dedicated her time to rearing their three children and promoting charitable causes. For Belgians, she was a model of elegance and courtesy.

At that period of history, the good customs, refined manners, and natural courtesy outlined in this manual were still practiced by many of the nobility of Europe and distinguished families of the United States. Such dignity of bearing and constant attention to protocol demanded a great discipline and sacrifice, and their good example set the tone to be followed not just by the elites, but by all the people. Their decorum and refinement elevated all – from the highest to the lowest.

Unfortunately, today such models are rare. Because of the Cultural Revolution and the Hollywood influence that has penetrated all classes of society, even the customs of the old families and elites have deteriorated. We believe, however, that courtesy should not be relegated to the world of museums and dust-heaps.

Seeing this charming picture, we have a strong yearning for that past where courtesy still reigned – and an even stronger hope that it will take its rightful place in society once again in the future. Toward that end, we all have a role to play.

In every Catholic home there is a king, the father of the family. He must take up the challenge to restore all things in Christ, beginning in his small kingdom. Presenting himself as serious, upright, and well-mannered, with the dignity that his social condition requires, he must assume the headship of his family and begin to guide it, inspired by the Catholic ideal from the past.

His wife must assist him by abandoning the Hollywood models and eschewing immoral fashions. Her goodness, gentility, and sacrifice will make her respected and admired by her spouse and children.

Adopting courteous ways of being, such men and women will become models for their own extended families, as well as for their parishes and communities. Striving for perfection in all things – their way of dress, speaking, and behaving – they will begin the work of restoration of a Christian culture. By their actions and attitudes, they will counter the revolutionary ways that are dominating society today. They will become true counter-revolutionaries.

We believe that there are many persons who, once they realize the importance of refined manners and dignified dress, will be willing to confront our false American myths and improve their behavior in the home.

They will want to be courteous to fulfill their obligation of charity and justice to others, showing them the respect and good treatment they deserve as creatures made in the image and likeness of God.

Catholics who love the hierarchy God placed in the universe will realize that, to uphold it in the family, they need to be more serious and follow an elevated protocol in their daily lives.

Experiencing that sweetness of life – the good fruit of a Christian culture – they will be willing to put aside some of the pragmatic and casual attitudes of our day and to strive for more consideration and distinction.

To behave without placing restraints on our spontaneity is to march down the slippery slope to barbarianism. It is to deny the fruit of hundreds of years of Catholic effort to correct bad human tendencies in order to build a Christian Civilization.

In the final analysis, there are two pathways: one that follows the way of courtesy, distinction, and morality, and another that leads to barbarianism, vulgarity, and immorality. The call to courtesy comes at a crucial moment in history, when vulgarity and immorality seem to be conquering every ambience and environment.

Now is the time to respond to this call and to change the course for the better. Our aim in writing this book has been to inspire families to answer this challenge to reinstate courtesy in the home.

* * *